D1591494

PROTECT YOURSELF

EVERY WOMAN'S SURVIVAL COURSE

PROTECT YOURSELF

EVERY WOMAN'S SURVIVAL COURSE

Judd Whitelaw

PHOTOGRAPHS BY
GEORGE WALTON

Javelin Books

POOLE · DORSET

*I would like to dedicate this book to two very
special people, whom I love very much,
and will remember always.*

*My daughter Tracey, who died in 1974
My brother Eddie, who died in 1973*

First published in the UK 1985 by Javelin Books,
Link House, West Street, Poole, Dorset BH15 1LL

Copyright © 1985 Judd Whitelaw

Distributed in the United States by
Sterling Publishing Co., Inc.,
2 Park Avenue, New York, NY 10016

British Library Cataloguing in Publication Data

Whitelaw, Judd
    Protect yourself : every woman's survival course.
    1. Self-defence for women
    I. Title   II. Walton, George
    613.6'6'088042   GV1111.5

ISBN 0 7137 1703 3

Typeset by Poole Typesetting (Wessex) Ltd, Bournemouth, Dorset

Printed in Great Britain by R. J. Acford Ltd, Chichester, Sussex.

Contents

Acknowledgements 6

Introduction 7

How To Use This Book 10

1 **Awareness** 11

2 **Warming Up–Twenty-Six Exercises** 15

3 **Using The Legs–Kicks** 38

4 **Running Escapes** 51

5 **Walking Escapes** 56

6 **Free Standing Holds–Strangles** 65

7 **Free Standing Holds–Hugs** 76

8 **Free Standing Holds–Arm Holds** 90

9 **Free Standing Holds–Wrist and Arm Locks** 103

10 **Up Against The Wall** 109

11 **Pulling Attacks** 119

12 **On The Floor** 133

13 **Personal Security and Travel** 150

Conclusion 155

Index 157

Acknowledgements

I should like to thank the many people and organisations who have contributed to the making of this book. Without their help, this book would not have been possible.

I would like to offer my special thanks to the following:

To my wife Gail – who changed my macho male attitude and convinced me that women were *not* second class citizens. I can mow the lawn now love.

To my children, Nicholas, Timothy and Clare – who didn't complain when I couldn't take them swimming. I can take you now.

To Master David Wongpaisan of Thailand – who in 1973, accepted a disabled man into his martial arts class and helped to mend his broken body.

To Nichola Boella – who, as a clinical psychologist, afforded us invaluable assistance.

To Judy Chamarette – who is one of the very few female Black Belt holders in Great Britain and who helped to design the Course.

To Graham Childs – who was 'the Attacker'. You can have a shave now Graham.

To Sue Sibley – who was 'the Victim' and also attended the very first Course.

To Peter H. Watson – who is responsible for the diagrams, and who suffered a dislocated shoulder at the hands of a 16-year-old girl during the last course.

To George Walton – who was our photographer.

To Yvonne Heather – who convinced me to put into print the results of my research, and whose efforts finally triumphed.

To the YMCA Surbiton, Surrey – who helped to make it possible and who continue to help in any way they can.

Finally, to the brothers – who continually seek more knowledge, and are members of the most exclusive club in the world.

Introduction

The Ladies Self Defence Association was first thought of in 1978, by a small group of self-defence/martial arts instructors. The aims of the Association were quite simple: to teach ladies what they needed to know, if, and when, they were confronted with the indignity of a personal attack. The reason behind a ladies-only class, was simple; very few ladies attended public, mixed, classes. The reasons for this were many. When questioning our ladies, several facts emerged. Most importantly, everyone said that they would like to learn some form of self defence. However, there were objections to open classes, one being that it took far too long for a woman to become *effective*. Another was the attitude of husbands and boyfriends who, though agreeing on the necessity for their loved ones to know something of self defence, didn't like the idea of their ladies being involved in mixed classes because of the amount of physical contact involved.

How then were we to overcome these two main objections? We could overcome the second very easily by opening a ladies-only class. The first objection however, 'it takes far too long for a woman to become *effective*', presented us with a much greater problem. It was felt by all concerned, that this was a very valid point. It does take a long time to develop the correct techniques, methods and style of any practitioner. This problem was not just peculiar to ladies but was the same for everyone.

So, what could we do to make ladies *effective* in a short time? We decided that we had first to discover what was happening in genuine attack situations. Were the ladies being held? Were they being pushed? Were they being thrown to the floor? The list was endless. We also had to learn a lot about the people who were doing the attacking. We had to find out whether there were any similarities involved in attack situations. We had to know how, who, when, where and why. If we could gather this information, then we could do something *positive*. We had to carry out a lot of research, use libraries, talk to victims and to a psychologist; we had to have the facts and the figures if we were going to help.

The amount of research constantly amazed us. It took almost 2 years to gather the information we needed. It was trial and error – what was useful, what was not? It was a long hard slog, but we eventually finished. We had the facts, we had the figures and now we could do something positive at last. We discovered almost immediately that the attackers did not use any particular style or technique when they attacked, but certain similarities did exist in most attacks. We looked at the similarities. To us, there seemed to be no difficulty in escaping, but of course we had all been practising for many years. We had to discover whether we could teach an absolute novice to use our methods *effectively*.

There was only one way to find out – *try!* We used friends and relatives, wives and girlfriends, mothers and daughters; in fact, just about every lady we knew was asked to take part in this experiment. We devised an introductory course to deal with the similarities of attack situations which we had encountered earlier. Instead of spending weeks or months concentrating on any one technique, as we would normally, we concentrated on *all* the similarities in attacks for a short time each week and introduced new methods of escape as the weeks went by.

We found that no one method of escape suited all of our ladies. To overcome this problem, we gave options of several different escapes for each type of attack. It worked! Each lady in turn chose the method of escape which complemented her best. We then gave our ladies even more options and asked them to choose not one but two different methods of escape for each type of attack.

It worked even better! This was a very important safety factor; if one chosen method didn't work first time, then there would still be an alternative. This then would be our formula. We would give several different options of escape for each attack situation and would encourage personal preference. In all the excitement, we had overlooked the most important factor. Would it work in a genuine attack situation? We studied this problem for some time and evaluated the facts.

The most useful ally we had was surprise. We had realised earlier in our research that an attacker effecting a serious attack expected the victim to be frightened. So, we told our ladies to appear to be frightened and followed the advice of the psychologist: catch the attacker offguard and make any defence count first time.

The only way to find out if our methods would work was to have our ladies attacked so we seconded the male novices we were teaching in our mixed classes and asked them to attack our ladies! Our attackers came in all shapes and sizes and it was an experience I shall never forget. Our attackers had no idea of what to expect as they had not been taught the escape methods taught to our ladies. They thought it would just be a bit of fun. How wrong they were! Our attackers were told to wear protective equipment: headguards, groinguards, elbow and knee protectors etc. Think about it – for probably the first time ever, a group of male attackers had to be protected from their victims.

The first attack was over in seconds. We had told our attacker to pin his victim to the wall and, if possible, remove the victim's clothing. Using one of our methods, our lady victim left the attacker clutching his groin on the floor. He couldn't help us any more. The other attackers were now starting to look a little worried. Another attacker was then asked to pin his victim to the floor and, once again, try to remove her clothing. Our lady victim quickly applied a wrist and arm lock to the attacker which forced him to the floor; she was standing, holding the attacker at her feet, completely at her mercy. The attacker was now the victim. Our lady victim looked at me and asked in what can only be described as a wickedly smug voice, 'How would you like this one, Judd, shaken or stirred?'

I had to answer quickly as the attacker was in a very distressed state, 'Just release him please'. The attacker was released and he walked away looking very sorry for himself. The rest of our attackers were now not so much worried as panic stricken. In fact, one of our volunteers decided that discretion was better than valour and refused to attack any of our ladies.

The next attacker was asked to pull his victim as though he was in a park or street, trying to pull her somewhere out of view. He pulled, she reacted, he went to hospital. The lady victim, using another of our methods, had completely winded him, leaving him gasping for breath and also breaking two of his ribs in the process. That is how it went on for the rest of the evening; from all of the similar-type attack situations, our ladies escaped unhurt. Unfortunately, the same can not be said for our volunteer attackers. After the first two injuries, I had to ask our ladies to take it easy as I did not want anyone else ending up in hospital. It was very difficult explaining to the hospital staff that our volunteer had just attacked a lady half his size and now required their skills to repair the damage. We, the instructors, were of course delighted. We had done it. We had taken a group of absolute novices and, in a very short time, made them effective.

After that first experimental group of ladies, we were then satisfied that we could do something positive. We began with an introductory 4-week course in Surrey. Once again, we used the same formula of instruction and once again we had the ladies attacked. The same thing happened – they all escaped without injury. After the initial introductory course, I decided to increase the length of the course to 6 rather than 4 weeks in order to give as many options as possible to our ladies. We have worked that way ever since, in and around London and, mainly, in the south of England. This book is all about our introductory 6 week course, although it is felt that ladies teaching themselves from this book should spend 12 rather than 6 weeks developing their techniques.

The book is divided into various stages, with easy to follow step-by-step photographs and diagrams. The first section deals with *awareness;* if you know the basic commonsense rules applicable to personal security, then, even without raising more than an eyebrow, it will make the odds against being attacked far greater.

Physical fitness is very important in self-defence practices: the fitter you are, the better your performance. It makes sense, doesn't it? No matter what you do, if you are fit and healthy, you will perform better. The exercises in Chapter 2 will help you get your body into shape for the techniques you are about to learn. Read it and follow it carefully.

Once you understand the fitness programme, you will be ready to start the course. You will have all of the more common types of attack explained to you, one by one. For each type of attack, you will be able to choose from various methods of escape. You must practise every option, then choose the two you like best. These should be the ones you find most effective for you personally. Do not accept the word of anyone else; if your chosen method of escape works for you, then that is the one to practise. What works for you may not work for anyone else. In like manner, what works for another may not work for you. Trust your own judgement; only you know your own capabilities and you are your own best critic. Be honest with yourself; does it work? Would another method be better? You must choose because, out on the streets, you may not have anyone to help you and it is you who ultimately decides how to deal with the situation. You are the one who is either going to get home safely or become just another statistic.

Use the exercise section to warm up and practise, practise, practise. Get your husband, boyfriend, father or uncle to help you. Anyone will do; explain to them what you are trying to achieve, get them involved and make them realise how important it is to you. Ask them how they would feel if you were the victim of a serious rape attack. Ask them if they would find that amusing. If we can re-educate the male population as to the real dangers involved then we can help ourselves to be safe.

Practise hard, as often as you can. Make it work for you, just as it has for so many others. Enjoy your course, and good luck.

Judd Whitelaw
Chief Instructor LSDA

How To Use This Book

The very first thing you are going to need is a partner. Once you have found someone to practise with, you can begin. The Introduction explained how we discovered that, although no two attacks are identical, in most there are similarities and each chapter deals with one of the similarities and one or more escape methods.

Each escape method is approached in three ways. First there is a brief description of what the attacker is trying to do and how the victim is dealing with the attack. The next part, How To Practise, explains fully how you can practise and escape from that particular type of attack. It describes with illustrations, the finer points of the escape method used. (It is always the finer points that make the escape method so very effective.) Thirdly, the main points of each escape method are presented in a summary. Each chapter has a conclusion in which I offer my final comments on whichever type of attack you are dealing with and also remind you of previous chapters which may be relevant. It is very important to read all the sections of each chapter *before* you start to practise, because the conclusion may also describe any dangers involved with a particular escape method. It is not that the escape methods are dangerous for you, but they can be dangerous for the attacker or, more importantly, your partner. Once you have read them all, you will have the relevant information you need for that type of attack. Armed with this, you can begin to practise.

Some of the escape methods need more practice than others, so if you find that a particular one is taking a long time to master, don't worry! It's the same for everyone at first. So long as you persevere and practise regularly, you'll get there in the end. If you give up on any of the escape methods you are practising, you may regret it later. After all, if you give up in practice, what will you do in a real attack?

Keep the book close at hand when you are practising, then, if you get confused, you can quickly find out where you are going wrong. Don't try to rush through an escape method; take your time and get it right. Practise every escape method until you feel 100% confident that you have it right. Then practise it again.

To get maximum benefit from the book, you should practise only one escape method at a time. When you have that one right, go on to the next, but don't forget what you have already done. You still have to practise all the escape methods regularly. Suppose that, during the first week, you have read and practised the methods in Chapters 3 and 4. You may feel ready to go on to Chapter 5. Ideally you should practise the methods in Chapters 3 and 4 *before* you start those in the new chapter. As you have already learned them, it shouldn't take too long to practise them.

By following this procedure, you will not forget what you have already done. So, in effect, your practice sessions will gradually get longer and longer. By the time you get to, say Chapter 8, your practice session would begin with all the escapes from Chapters 2 to 7. Then you would continue with those in Chapter 8 in the normal way. Don't forget, all the time you are practising, you are getting fitter and healthier and, because you are taking your time, and building up gradually, your body will easily cope with each new escape method, as it is added to your practice sessions. Take your time. Build up gradually. You *can* do it. Good luck!

1 Awareness

In order to increase the odds *against* being attacked, it is very important to realise that it doesn't always happen to somebody else. It really can happen to *you*.

Just take a look at these facts and figures for the United Kingdom:

FACT: There were 1,336 rapes reported to the Police in 1982.[1]
FACT: There were 412 convictions for rape in 1982.[1]
FACT: 50% of all rape victims are known to the attacker.[2]
FACT: 83% of all rape victims are in the 13-29 age group.[2]
FACT: 60% of all rape attacks happen indoors.[3]
FACT: Approximately 75% of attacks are not reported to the Police.[3]

When considering this information, it would appear that there were 5,344 attacks in 1982 and only 412 convictions, i.e. one conviction for nearly every thirteen attacks. It makes you shudder to think that, if thirteen men were to attack one woman each, only one man would be convicted of his crime.

The figures[4] for the United States are just as alarming:

FACT: An estimated 78,918 forcible rapes were reported to law enforcement agencies in 1983. This is equivalent to one forcible rape every 7 minutes and represents 6% of the total number of violent crimes.
FACT: In 1983, an estimated 66 women out of every 100,000 were reported as rape victims. This breaks down into: 76 per 100,000 in metropolitan state areas; 41 per 100,000 outside metropolitan areas and 29 per 100,000 in rural counties.
FACT: In 1983, 50% of men arrested for forcible rape were under 25 years old and 25% were between 18 and 22 years old. 50% were black and 49% were white.
FACT: The geographical distribution of forcible rapes in 1983 was: southern states (the region with the largest population) 35% (67 per 100,000); western states 26% (86 per 100,000); north-central states 23% (60 per 100,000); north-eastern states 16% (51 per 100,000).
FACT: More forcible rapes occur during the summer months.
FACT: The number of forcible rapes, in common with other crimes, is increasing.
FACT: Approximately 45% of forcible rapes are not reported.

In view of all this information, what can we do to prevent such an experience happening to *you?*

Well, you could start by following these nine simple rules:

1. Don't walk alone late at night; get someone to meet you if possible.
2. Don't take short cuts through unlit areas; stay where it is busy and walk in the centre of the pavement.
3. Don't dawdle.
4. Don't travel in empty train carriages. Stay in the crowd.
5. Don't open your front door without knowing who is outside. Use a safety chain or a spy hole in the door.
6. Don't allow strangers into your home without proof of identity.
7. Don't drive your car alone without locking the doors.
8. Don't give lifts to strangers or men you know only slightly.

1 Official Home Office Criminal Statistics figure.
2 *Home Office Research Study* No. 54. Published in 1979. (Latest study)
3 Information supplied by Rape Crisis Centre, London.
4 Book of Criminal Justice Statistics 1981.
5 Uniform Crime Reports 1984.

9. Don't accept lifts from men either, unless you know them really well.

It is commonsense really and the number of attacks on women would drop dramatically if they all followed these nine simple rules. Follow the rules and you lessen the chances of attack; ignore them and you are just as prone to attack as everyone else.

How else can you lessen the chances of attack? Have a look at this. 'Of the 258 lone attacks, i.e. by a single attacker, there were only three cases of attacks on two women together in single incidents'. Work it out for yourself. If you are out with a friend, you lessen the chances of attack by about 98.8%. Read on, it is getting still better. 'The highest number of incidents take place on the following evenings: Thursday, Friday, Saturday and Sunday, and are usually alcohol-oriented'.[1]

We are not suggesting that you lock yourselves up at home on those evenings, but if you know when you are most at risk you can act accordingly. We have already reduced the chances of attack very considerably.

Is there anything more we can possibly do? Well, how about finding out something about the attackers? If you are confronted with an attacker, what is the best and safest thing to do to escape without injury? Understanding the attacker can help very much indeed when you are in this situation and the following information should be useful:

FLASHERS: are not usually dangerous. These people get their kicks from the shock they inflict on their victims and normally run off to avoid capture. However, it is always best to assume that even a flasher could be dangerous if provoked. *Don't* be brave, *run* – preferably into a more crowded area.

HANDBAG-SNATCHERS: Usually grab and run. They don't want problems. If you fight the snatcher you will panic him and this could cause him to be more violent towards *you*. He will usually be in his teens or early twenties and, being young and strong, will be able to

inflict injury. (If carrying a handbag, why not keep your cash in your pocket?).

RAPE ATTACKERS: Most women try to fight off their attacker/s and it is very difficult to say whether this is good or bad. Some attackers may well be fought off by strong resistance, but others may well become more excited by the fight. One must decide for oneself if the attacker can be fought off and act accordingly. One thing is certain: futile blows are a waste of time; if you decide to fight make it count.

If you can stun an attacker for just 10 to 20 seconds then this will give you time to escape and get help. Screaming as loudly as you can should attract attention but, sadly, may not get help. The public all too often just don't want to get involved in a situation that may cause them to get injured. Rather than screaming 'RAPE!' As loudly as you can scream 'FIRE!' This usually brings people out, for fear they may be in danger themselves. An attacker will usually run off to avoid capture when people start to open doors etc, and take an interest in what is going on.

Generally speaking, you must use your own instinct for survival to escape; catch your attacker off guard and surprise him. Your own wits are sometimes enough to escape and, of course, being able to run.

You now have some idea about the nature of attackers and this should help you a lot in deciding how to face an attack if threatened.

Armed with all this information, you may well be saying to yourself, 'Surely I can't be attacked'. Sorry, but you can. You see, unfortunately, rapists and sex offenders don't wear uniforms and, as you have already read, 50% of all victims are known to their attacker. Attackers are often friends of the victim's husband, brother or sister. In fact, an attacker may be anybody you already know. What can you do in this case? Obviously you can try and talk your way out of the situation. Use you own wits: tell him it's the wrong time of the month, tell him you're ill, tell him anything you like, but if all else fails, you have to make a decision.

You have several options. Only *you* can decide what course of action to take. You could try to fight him off but remember: 'Some attackers may well be fought off

1 *Medical Science and Law* 1981, vol. 21, No.1.
Flashers, Handbag Snatchers, Rape Attackers. Based on information provided by N. Boella (Clinical Psychologist).

by a strong resistance, but others may well become more excited by the fight'. So, trying to fight him off may well work. On the other hand, it may not. You have to decide. Are you capable of fighting him off? Or will you make the situation worse? 'One thing is certain, futile blows are a waste of time, if you decide to fight make it count. You may decide not to fight and then report the crime to the Police. He'll get 20 years for this you may well think? Really? Have a look at these UK conviction rates:

FACT: Offenders aged 17 to 20. 95% received sentences of no more than 5 years. (Less than 2 years: 31%. More than 2 but less than 5 years: 64%. Total: 95%.[1])
FACT: Offenders aged over 21. 73% received sentences of less than 5 years. (Less than 2 years: 15%. More than 2 but less than 5 years: 58%. Total: 73%.[1])

So you may well report the crime to the Police, and you may well get the attacker convicted, but it is just as possible that you may not get a conviction. Why not? Look:

FACT: There were 1,336 rapes reported to the Police in 1983; there were 412 convictions.[2]

Why do you suppose the conviction rate isn't higher? Well it is obvious that a rapist is not going to admit his crime. He knows that there is a possibility of receiving the maximum penalty, which is *life*. He is going to argue in court, because he does not want to run the risk of going to prison.

What then is the problem? Could it have something to do with the Law? Surely a woman who has suffered the indignity of a rape attack can get the attacker convicted? Surely a woman can get the sympathy of the jury? Let's have a look at those three questions:
*When a rape attack is reported to the Police and the case eventually goes to Court, there are three main points which have to be proved to the jury:

1. The identity of the attacker. This is not usually a

problem, simply because of the close proximity of the attacker to the victim at the time the crime occurred.
2. That the crime occurred. The Law defines rape as follows: sexual intercourse with a woman who at the time of intercourse does not consent to it.
3. Intention. In bringing an attacker to court, the victim must prove beyond all question that the attacker intended to commit rape. This is usually the most difficult part of the trial. Because of the serious nature of the crime, a woman can expect the accusation to be fiercely contested. The attacker's Counsel can be expected to do his utmost to get an acquittal for his client. This is usually the most upsetting part of the trial for the victim. Counsel for the Defence will cross-examine severely the victim's accusation.*

So there you are, the plain truth of the matter is that it is very difficult to get a conviction for rape. But it's your choice, only *you* can decide. So what else could you do? Perhaps you could be one of the 75% or so who *don't* report the crime to the Police? Once again it's your choice. You are aware of all the facts and figures. You are aware of the difficulties. You are aware that you are on your own. Only *you* can decide what to do and none of it seems very fair. No matter what you decide, you are going to have to live with it for the rest of your life – or maybe not? How many times have you read in the newspapers of the police finding the body of a woman who had been sexually assaulted? What is sometimes questionable is, are the Police looking for a murderer who sexually assaulted the victim or for a rapist who murdered his victim? It is amazing that the legal system will pull out all the stops to capture a murderer and, once captured, he may get a life sentence. The media will give their full support to the Police to help in the apprehension of a killer but a victim of a rape attack hardly warrants a few lines in the local paper. And yet a convicted rapist can receive the same life sentence.

In practice, hardly any rapist convicted in the UK receives the maximum custodial sentence. It seems very strange that our society can demand similar custodial offences for rapists and murderers alike and yet the sentence for murder is applied as for a crime against

---

1 *Home Office Research Study* No. 54. Published in 1979.
2 Official Home Office Criminal Statistics figure.

*Source: London Weekend Television's *Weekend World*. Broadcast on 14 February 1982.

society and civilisation and the sentence for rape seems to be applied as for an error on a man's (or more usually a woman's) part. Could this be because our legal system is male dominated and that few men really understand the true effects a rape attack has on a woman?

Until such time as the male mind is broadened to cease considering women as second-class citizens, the onus is on women to make themselves aware of what actually happens in a rape/sexual attack. If you know this, you can learn how to escape from an attacker. You can learn how 'If you decide to fight, to make it count'. That is what this book is all about, telling you what is likely to happen and how to escape if all else fails. From

the office wolf to the groping late-night drunk who can turn a walk home into a nightmare, from the hand-on-the-knee macho man to the more serious, pinned-to-the-wall or floor rape attacker, it is possible to escape, and you can teach yourself how with the help of this book. Whether you are dragged along the floor by your feet, or held by your arms in a bear hug, you *can* escape. It's up to you. You can put this book down and ignore it, or you can do something positive and read on.

It is easy to follow, with a step-by-step guide to make it simple, and it may save you a lot of suffering and pain.

Be aware and follow the rules, it will help to keep you safe.

2 Warming Up- Twenty-Six Exercises

This chapter deals with your body. In order to achieve the best possible results, we have to tone our bodies. As with all manner of physical activity, you have to start slowly and gradually to build up your body. If you are in any doubt about how your body is going to react to exercise, then go and see your doctor! Take the book with you and show him/her what you want to do.

Before you start to practise the escape methods in the following chapters, it is very important that you warm up first. If you don't you will start to suffer from pulled muscles and possibly strains and similar injuries. By warming up, you increase your heart rate and blood is pumped through your body a little more quickly, carrying more oxygen to your muscles, thus helping to prevent injury. It also serves to exercise your lungs and loosen up your body all round. No matter what you do for a living, or your walk of life, if you are fit and healthy you will perform better.

It is advisable to wear loose clothing when exercising; a track suit is ideal and a pair of well-cushioned trainers or running shoes provide excellent cushioning and protection for the feet. Once you are suitably dressed, you are ready to begin but remember these few things while you are warming up:

1. *Don't* try and rush through all of the exercises too quickly. Start slowly and gently, and gradually build up.

2. If you get out of breath, *stop*. You've overdone it, probably by starting too quickly.

3. If you feel pain in any part of your body *stop*. You have probably overdone it and more than likely pulled a muscle.

4. If you feel sick or dizzy, *stop*. You have overdone it, probably by going too quickly.

5. Listen to your body; it will tell you when it wants to stop. If you have any doubt whatsoever, *stop*.

6. Remember, the exercises are designed to tone you up. They will no doubt be hard work at first, but keep at it; you'll get there in the end. It's hard for everyone at first, especially if you're not involved in any other sports activity.

There are twenty-six exercises altogether, but, you are not recommended to attempt all of them on the first day. Start by trying the odd numbers on the first day, then the even numbers on the second day. On the third day, *don't* practise. Give your body a chance to rest, especially if it is not accustomed to exercise. I have designed a chart for the benefit of the ladies who are not accustomed to physical exercise. Those ladies who are in top form physically should be able to decide for themselves how much to do and act accordingly.

EXERCISE No. 1
JUMPING ON THE SPOT

Stand up straight and hold your arms out to the sides at an angle of about 45°. Now, raise your heels off the floor and stand on the balls of your feet. Once in this position, jump up and down, jumping approximately 6 inches off the floor to begin with, then increasing the height of your jump gradually.

Your arms are held out to the sides to aid your balance but, once you have the hang of it, you can keep your arms into your sides if you wish. You should jump up and down on the balls of your feet. Don't put your heels onto the floor until you have finished the exercise.

This exercise will help to strengthen your calf muscles and, to some extent, your ankles.

Do up to approximately 20 jumps.

DAY NUMBER	EXERCISE NUMBERS	PRACTISE ESCAPES
01	Odd Numbers only	Yes
02	Even Numbers only	Yes
03	Rest, don't practise	No
04	1 to 6 plus remaining odd Numbers	Yes
05	1 to 6 plus remaining even Numbers	Yes
06	Rest, don't practise	No
07	1 to 12 plus remaining odd Numbers	Yes
08	1 to 13 plus remaining even Numbers	Yes
09	Even numbers only	Yes
10	Rest, don't practise	No
11	1 to 14 plus remaining odd Numbers	Yes
12	1 to 17 plus remaining even Numbers	Yes
13	1 to 12 plus remaining odd Numbers	Yes
14	Rest, don't practise	No
15	1 to 14 plus remaining odd Numbers	Yes
16	1 to 21 plus remaining even Numbers	Yes
17	1 to 24 plus remaining odd Numbers	Yes
18	1 to 21 plus remaining even Numbers	Yes
19	Rest, don't practise	No
20	1 to 22 plus remaining odd Numbers	Yes
21	1 to 26	Yes
22	1 to 26	Yes
23	1 to 26	Yes
24	Rest, don't practise	No
25	1 to 26	Yes
26	1 to 26	Yes
27	1 to 26	Yes
28	1 to 26	Yes
29	As you feel from now on	As you feel

Warming Up Exercise Chart

EXERCISE No. 2
STAR JUMPS

Start by standing up straight, arms by your sides and feet together.

Jump up and, at the same time, part your feet sideways. As you are jumping up and parting your feet, raise both your arms out to the sides in a circular motion, so that your hands meet above your head. Land with your feet apart and your hands above your head. Jump up again and return to the starting position. Try to do this exercise on the balls of your feet; it will make for a softer landing.

This exercise does many things for your body. It helps to improve your co-ordination, increases your cardiovascular performance (heart and lungs), strengthens your thighs and loosens your hips and shoulders. There are many other benefits but they are far too many to mention.

Each set comprises 1 complete exercise.

Do approximately 5 to 20 sets.

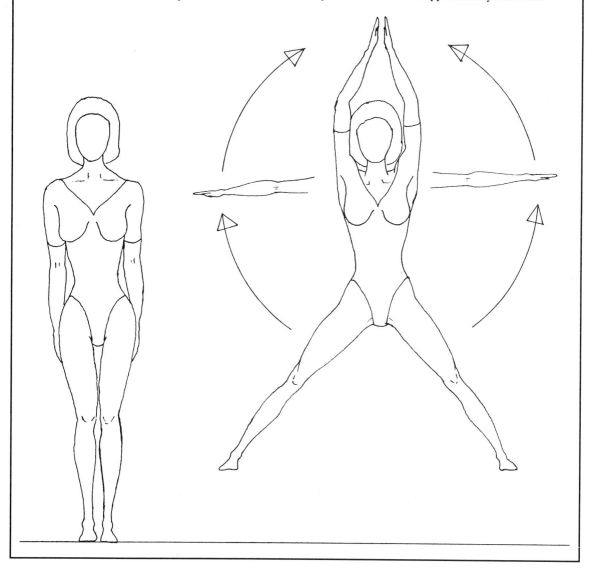

EXERCISE No. 3
SQUATS

Start by standing up straight, arms by your sides and feet together.

Swing your arms forward and above your head in a circular motion. Once your arms are above your head, swing them back down to your sides and at the same time bend your knees and squat down. Then stand up and raise your arms above your head again. When you are standing with your arms above your head, swing your arms back to the starting position.

This exercise, like the last one, does many things for your body. It improves your co-ordination and cardiovascular system, strengthens your legs and loosens your shoulders. As with the last exercise, there are far too many other benefits to mention.

5 to 20 sets.

EXERCISE No. 4
WAIST STRETCHING

Start with your feet wide apart, toes pointing forward and body upright.

Put your right arm behind your head and *gently* stretch down to your left, trying to touch your left ankle with your left hand. Gently stretch down 3 times and come up to the starting position; stretch to the other side 3 times.

This exercise helps to improve your suppleness. It stretches your waist and back and also helps to stretch your legs.

3 to 10 sets.

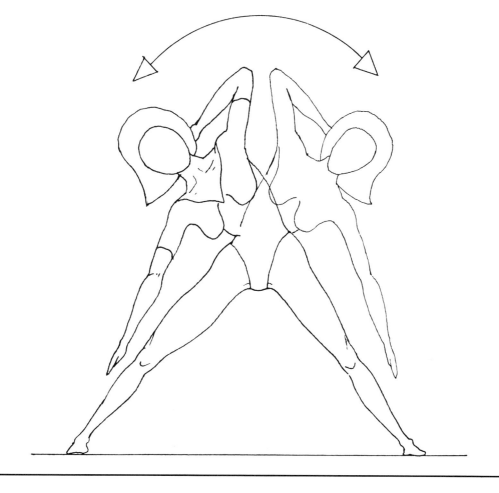

EXERCISE No. 5
WAIST AND BACK

Start with your feet wide apart, body upright, toes pointing forward.

Gently bend forward from the waist and try to touch the floor behind your heels. Try to touch the floor twice, i.e. bend first, then try to touch the floor behind your heels – *one, two*. Then come up and place your hands on your hips and *gently* bend backwards from the waist. Bend backwards twice, i.e. *one, two*. Then return to the starting position.

This exercise is mainly to improve your suppleness. It gently stretches your back and tummy muscles and also helps to loosen your hips. It also helps to stretch your legs and, to some extent, improves your sense of balance.

2 to 5 sets.

EXERCISE No. 6
NECK

These neck exercises should be practised *very slowly*. Do *not* rush through them because, if you do, you may jar your neck.

Stand up straight with your hands on your hips, feet slightly apart. Look straight ahead and turn your head left, then right.

Standing in the same position, take your head down, so that your chin reaches your chest, then take your head backwards as far as it will go.

Take your chin down to your chest and rotate your head in a complete circle, clockwise then anti-clockwise.

Take your head backwards and move your head left and right, as though trying to touch your shoulders with your ears.

All of these exercises are designed to loosen your neck and shoulders. Care should be taken when practising them. Go through them very gently and slowly.

If you start to feel dizzy then, you are going too quickly; *stop* and wait for the dizziness to go.

1 to 4 sets each exercise.

EXERCISE No. 7
ARMS AND SHOULDERS

Stand up straight, arms by your sides, feet slightly apart.

Swing your arms in outward circles, 4 times. Then reverse and swing your arms in inward circles 4 times.

This exercise is mainly for your arms and shoulders. It helps to loosen them up and, to some extent, improves your co-ordination.

2 to 4 sets.

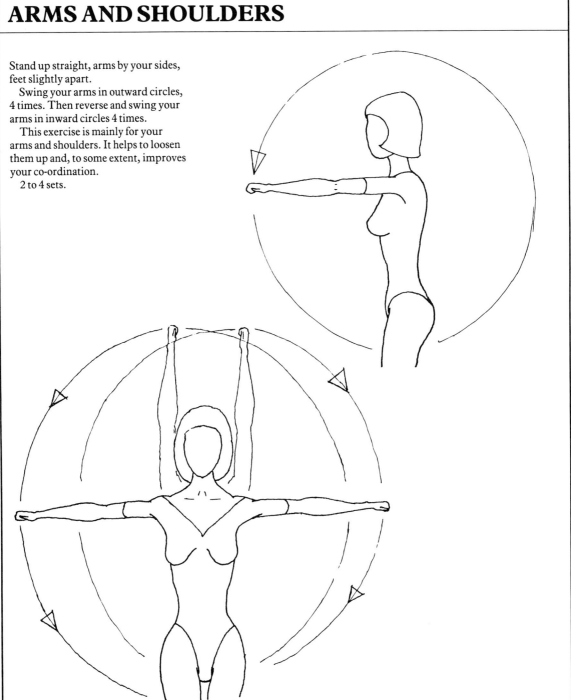

EXERCISE No. 8
CARDIOVASCULAR

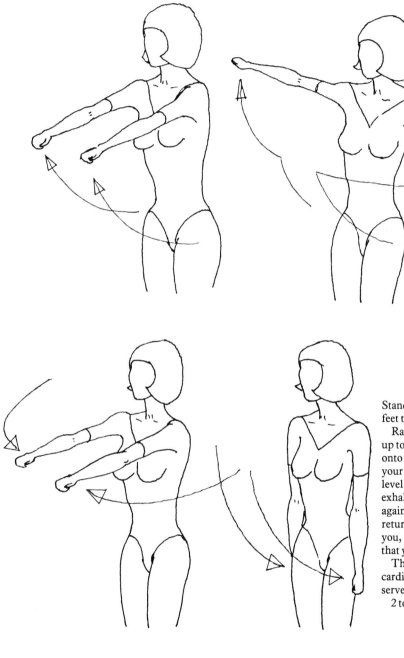

Stand up straight, arms by your sides, feet together.

Raise your arms in front of you, just up to shoulder height. Then stand onto the balls of your feet and swing your arms backwards, still at shoulder level. As you swing your arms back, exhale. Now swing your arms forward again and breathe in. When you have returned your arms back in front of you, put them back by your sides, so that you are in the start position again.

This exercise is primarily for the cardiovascular system but will also serve to improve your co-ordination.

2 to 4 sets.

EXERCISE No. 9
CO-ORDINATION

Stand up straight, feet slightly apart. Raise your right arm above your head and keep your left arm by your side. This is the starting position.

Take your right arm downwards to your side and, at the same time, raise your left arm above your head. Both of your arms are moving in a circular motion at the same time but they are moving in opposite directions. Do 4 circles with each arm then, reverse the direction. Do 4 circles with each arm but in opposite directions.

This exercise really improves your co-ordination dramatically. It also serves as a shoulder-loosening exercise.

4 to 10 sets.

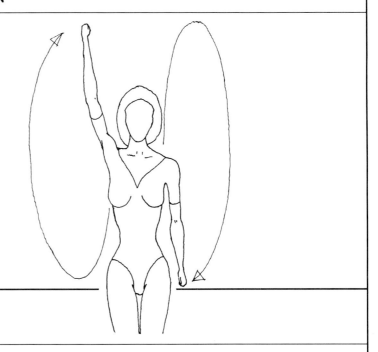

EXERCISE No. 10
TOE TOUCHING

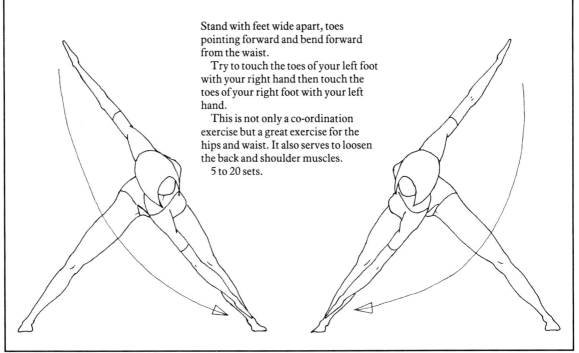

Stand with feet wide apart, toes pointing forward and bend forward from the waist.

Try to touch the toes of your left foot with your right hand then touch the toes of your right foot with your left hand.

This is not only a co-ordination exercise but a great exercise for the hips and waist. It also serves to loosen the back and shoulder muscles.

5 to 20 sets.

EXERCISE No. 11
CROSS BENDS

Stand with feet wide apart, toes pointing forward, body upright and cross your arms in front of you. This is the starting position.

Uncross your arms and swing them in a circular motion above your head. When your arms are above your head, bend forward from the waist and try to touch the floor behind your heels. Then raise your body and swing your arms back in a full circle, so that you move back to the starting position. As you bend forward from the waist, exhale. As you come back up, breathe in.

This is a cardiovascular and co-ordination exercise. It is also a great stretching exercise for your back and hips. In all, an excellent all-rounder.

4 to 10 sets.

EXERCISE No. 12
TORSO ROUNDS

With your feet wide apart and hands above your head, bend forward from the waist. This is the starting position.

Gently rotate your torso (upper body) in large circles, first clockwise, then anti-clockwise. Do one circle one way, then one the other way.

This exercise is great for the hips, waist and back. It will improve the suppleness of your back, hips and waist and will also serve to improve your sense of balance.

4 to 10 sets.

EXERCISE No. 13
KNEES

Stand with your feet together, bend forward from the waist and place your hands onto your knees. This is the starting position.

Bend your knees and try to touch your heels with your bottom. Try to touch your heels *twice,* with your bottom, i.e. bend your knees then *touch* and *touch* again. Then return to the starting position. When you have returned to the starting position, gently push back on your knees twice. That completes 1 set.

2 to 4 sets.

EXERCISE No. 13A
KNEES

Take up the same starting position.
   Gently rotate your knees in a full circle. First one way, then the other. That completes 1 set.
   2 to 4 sets.

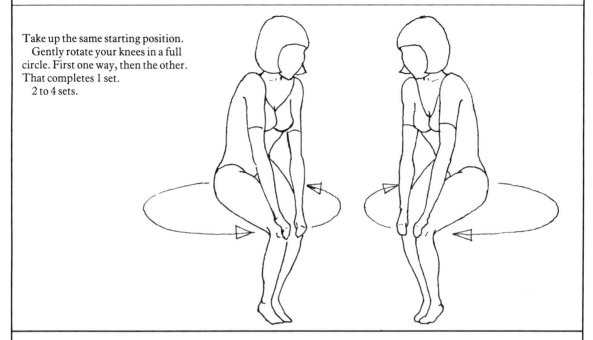

EXERCISE No. 14
SQUAT STRETCHES

With the body upright, stand with your feet wide apart and toes pointing forward. This is the starting position.
   Keeping your right leg straight, raise the toes of your right foot so that they point upwards. Now, gently bend your *left* leg so that you squat down. Keep both of your heels on the floor as you squat down; don't raise them. Try to touch the floor with your bottom. Get as low as you possibly can without losing your balance or raising your heels. *Hold* that position for 5 to 20 seconds. Then repeat on the other side in exactly the same way.
   You may find that it helps to lean between your legs as you squat down.
   This exercise is mainly a stretching exercise. It stretches the hamstrings in your legs and the tendons around your knees. Do it gently and don't overdo it.
   No more than 2 sets of 5 to 20 seconds.

EXERCISE No. 15
BALANCE

Stand up straight and hold your arms out to the sides, parallel to the floor. This is the starting position.

Raise your right knee in front of you and rotate it in large circles, first clockwise then anti-clockwise. Do four circles in each direction. Then change legs and repeat the exercise with your left leg. As your sense of balance improves, you should be able to do this exercise without raising your arms out to the sides.

This exercise does several things. It not only improves your sense of balance and co-ordination but also serves to loosen your hips and improve your suppleness.

Each set comprises 8 circles with each leg: 4 circles one way then 4 circles the other way.

2 to 4 sets.

EXERCISE No. 15A
BALANCE

Take up the same starting position.
    Swing your legs up in front of you as high as they will go. Try to keep both of your legs straight as you swing them. Swing your right leg up 3 times and then your left. Each set comprises 6 leg swings: 3 with your right leg and 3 with your left.
    As well as improving your sense of balance and loosening your hips, this exercise also helps to strengthen your thighs (upper leg muscles).
    2 to 4 sets.

EXERCISE No. 16
PUSH UPS

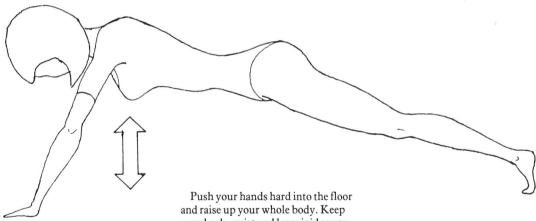

Lie face down on the floor. Plant the palms of your hands firmly onto the floor, level with your shoulders. Keep your body straight and your feet together. The balls of your feet should be on the floor. This is the starting position.

Push your hands hard into the floor and raise up your whole body. Keep your back, waist and legs rigid as you raise your body. You are lifting your body with only your arms.
    Exhale as you push up. Breathe in as you go back down.
    This exercise is mainly for the cardiovascular system but also serves to tone your shoulders, back and legs.

When you are lowering your body back to the starting position, go down slowly. Don't just drop back onto the floor.
    Each set comprises 1 push up and 1 lowering down.
    5 to 20 sets.

EXERCISE No. 17
SIT UPS

Lie down, back to the floor, with hands behind your head, knees raised 2 to 3 inches off the floor and your heels on the floor. This is the starting position.

Try to raise your torso up and touch your knees with your head. If you can't raise your torso, don't worry. Get someone to hold your feet for you; this will make it much easier. As you progress, you will be able to do it without your feet being held. As you raise your torso, you should keep your heels on the floor. Each set comprises one torso raise up and one torso lowering down. As you lower your torso down, don't let it just drop. Lower it slowly down to the floor.

This exercise is for the abdominal muscles (tummy) and will firm and flatten them in next to no time.

5 to 20 sets.

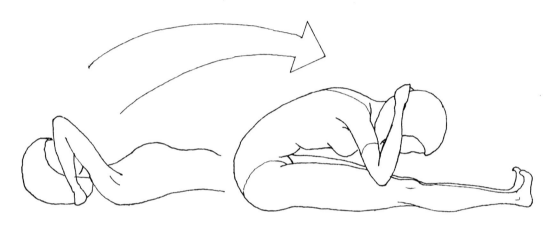

The next 7 exercises require a partner. If you have no partner then, under *no* circumstances, should you try to improvise or you will probably hurt yourself.

If you are without a partner, go on to Exercises No. 25 and 26, then continue in the normal way.

EXERCISE No. 18
DOGGY SIT UPS

Your partner kneels on the floor, doggy-style, with head tucked well into the chest, and arms locked at the elbow.

Sit on your partner's back, as shown in the diagram. Lock your feet into your partner's thighs and place your hands behind your head. Check with the diagram to make certain that you are in the correct position. This is the starting position.

Now lower your torso gently down to your partner's back, so that you are back to back. Once you are back to back, raise your torso back up into the starting position again. That is one set.

If you find this exercise causes back pain, *stop*. As with all the exercises, this is meant to improve your performance, not hurt you. There may be discomfort in the beginning, but you should not feel pain.

This exercise will get rid of excess fat and really firm your tummy and front thighs.

3 to 20 sets.

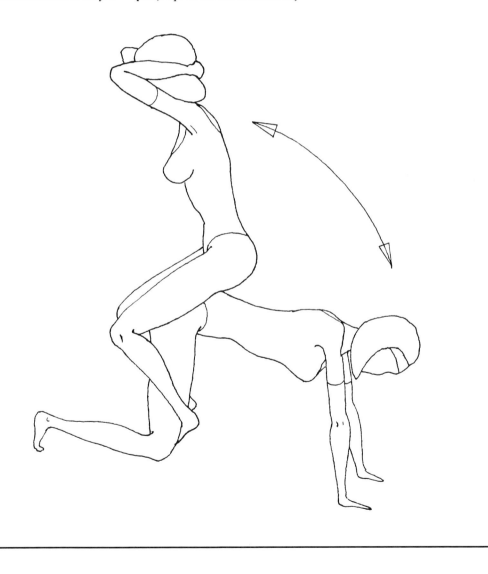

EXERCISE No. 19
SPINAL STRETCHING

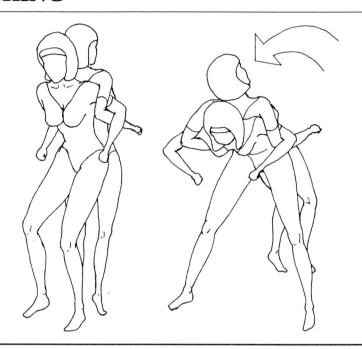

Stand back to back with your partner and link arms, exactly as shown in the diagram.

The lower partner should lift the upper partner's feet off the floor. This is done by gently leaning forward. The upper partner should completely relax once in the correct position (see diagram). If you feel any pain at all then *stop*. This exercise is to be done very gently. Hold the relaxed position for 5 to 20 seconds; the lower partner should then gently stand upright again. Don't stand up too quickly; if you do, you may lose your balance and fall down.

This exercise is for increasing the suppleness in your back. It should gently stretch the muscles in your back and tummy, making your back more manoeuvrable.

2 sets of 5 to 20 seconds.

EXERCISE No. 20
BACK STRETCHING

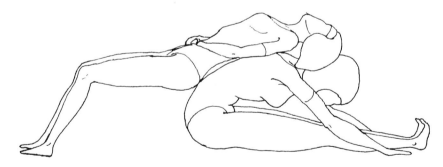

Exercise No. 19 stretched your back in one direction and this exercise complements it. We are now going to stretch in the opposite direction.

Sit down, back to back with your partner. Keeping your legs straight; curl your toes towards your head. Then lean forward from the waist and try to touch your knees with your head. Your partner can lie on your back if you like, just as shown in the diagram. If your partner lies on your back, try to relax and let your partner's weight take your head down to your knees gently. Hold this position for 5 to 20 seconds. After this time, your partner should leave your back very slowly and gently. If your partner leaves your back too quickly, you may spring up and pull a muscle. Come up from this exercise *very slowly*.

This exercise has the same benefits as Exercise No. 19.

2 sets of 5 to 20 seconds.

EXERCISE No. 21
STAND UPS

Sit down, back to back with your partner and link arms, just as for Exercise No. 19. Your legs should be straight. This is the starting position.

From the starting position, pull your feet in towards your bottom and plant them firmly onto the floor. Both partners should be in the position shown in the diagram: back to back, knees raised and feet planted firmly onto the floor. From this position, both of you should use your legs to push yourselves into your partner's back. You should both push together. The result of pushing together will be that you will both stand up. When you are both standing up, sit down again, still with arms linked. When you are both sitting down again, put your legs out straight so that you are in the starting position again. This movement and returning to the starting position again comprises 1 set.

This exercise strengthens your lower back and your legs.

2 to 10 sets.

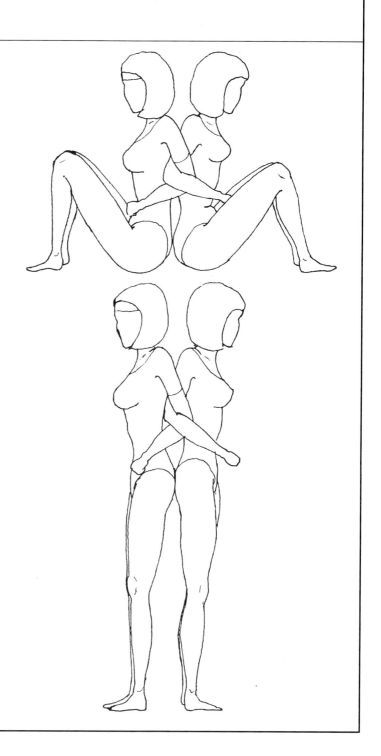

EXERCISE No. 22
FORWARD LEG STRETCHING

Stand facing your partner. This is the starting position.

Get your partner to hold your left leg. Your partner should then raise your leg, but not too much, just enough for you to feel the thigh muscles begin to tighten slightly. Both of your legs should be kept straight. Concentrate on your supporting leg; make sure it is straight. Hold that position for 5 to 20 seconds. Then, if you can, get your partner to raise your leg a little more and hold that position for the same time. Do this once more, if you can, and while your partner is raising your leg, try to lean forward and place your head onto your raised knee.

This exercise may feel uncomfortable but it should not feel painful. If it hurts, *stop;* you've overdone it. If you feel a burning sensation in your supporting leg, then stop; you have held the position for too long. This exercise should be done slowly and gently. Discomfort is to be expected, but not pain. When you have completed stretching your left leg, then stretch your right leg in the same way for the same time. Your partner should lower your leg slowly and gently; don't lower it quickly. This exercise is obviously for stretching your leg muscles. It will help you considerably when, later on, you start to practise the various leg techniques. It is a superb exercise for increasing the fluidity in your legs and it should not be very long before you find that you can raise your feet above your head.

Each set comprises raising each leg to 3 different heights. At each height, the position should be held for 5 to 20 seconds.

1 set only.

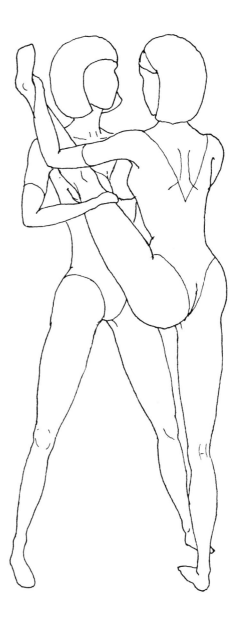

EXERCISE No. 23
SIDEWAYS STRETCHING

Look at the diagram and sit down facing your partner. Your legs should be held wide apart with your toes curled towards your head. Your partner, facing you, places his/her feet, just below the sides of your knees and holds your wrists. This is the starting position.

Your partner, who is holding your wrists, gently pulls you forward from the waist. At the same time, you should concentrate on trying to get your head to the floor. This exercise should be done in 3 stages, so that you get a little lower each time. Each lowering stage, should be held for 5 to 20 seconds. It is very important that you relax when doing this exercise. If your muscles are tense, then it will make the exercise much more difficult for you. If you stay relaxed, it makes it much easier. When you have completed the exercise, you should come up *slowly* and then gently put your feet back together.

This exercise, like Exercise No. 22, will increase the fluidity in your legs considerably and it should not be too long before you can get your head all the way onto the floor. It may cause you some discomfort, but it should not cause pain. If you do find that you are in pain, then *stop,* but remember to come up slowly. If you come up too quickly you may pull a muscle.

Each set comprises 3 lowering stages. Each lowering stage should be held for 5 to 20 seconds.

This exercises both legs at the same time.

1 set only.

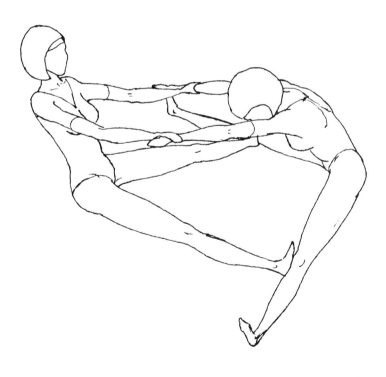

EXERCISE No. 24
BACKWARD LEG STRETCHING

Look at the diagram. One partner stretches while the other supports. The stretching partner places her right shoulder against the wall. Her supporting leg is no more than 12 to 18 inches away from the wall. The toes of her supporting leg should point towards the wall, as though forming a letter 'T' with the wall. The stretching partner now gets her supporting partner to gently raise her *left* leg. The toes of the raised leg should point to the floor. The stretching partner should look across her *left* shoulder, towards her raised *left* heel. Try to keep your torso upright to the wall

when you stretch. This exercise is done in three stages, raising your leg a little higher in each stage. When you have completed all three stages, your partner should lower your raised leg slowly. This exercise may cause discomfort but shouldn't cause pain. If it causes pain, *stop*, but remember to lower your leg slowly. If you lower your leg too quickly, you may pull a muscle.

This exercise is another which increases the fluidity in your legs. When you have completed this exercise, you will have stretched your legs in 3 different directions: forwards,

sidewards and backwards. This exercise complements Exercises No. 22 and 23. When you have completed all 3 exercises, your legs should feel very loose. This is because you have stretched them in a way that they are not used to. The more you stretch, the better your leg techniques will be later on.

Each set comprises 3 different height stages for each leg. Each height stage should be held for 5 to 20 seconds. Obviously both legs should be stretched.

1 set only.

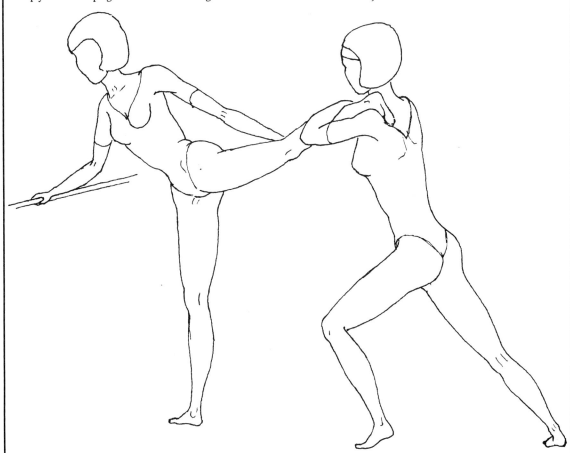

EXERCISE No. 25
COMPLEMENTARY STRETCHING

This exercise complements Exercise No. 24. Start by standing with your feet together and then gently bend forward from the waist. This is the starting position.

Grip your ankles or lower calves, with both of your hands. Then gently pull your head in towards your knees. Hold this position for 5 to 20 seconds. Then release your grip and gently stand up straight. That completes 1 set.

Exercise No. 24 has stretched your legs backwards; this exercise complements it by stretching your legs, and back, in the opposite direction. When you have completed this exercise, you will feel even more supple than you did before. This exercise stretches both legs at the same time.

1 or 2 sets.

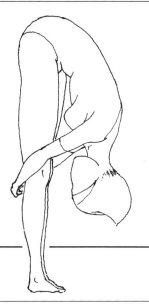

EXERCISE No. 26
HIPS LOOSENING

Stand up straight, feet together and hold your arms out to the sides. This is the starting position.

Raise each knee, in turn, up to your chest. Keep the foot of the raised knee tightly tucked in to your bottom, as though you raise your leg in a letter 'V' The top lefthand side of the 'V' would be your left hip and vice versa. The diagram shows the correct position of the raised knee.

This exercise adds the final polish to the stretching exercises you have already completed. It loosens your hips and adds to the already increased fluidity of your legs.

Each set comprises 4 alternate knee raises.

2 to 5 sets.

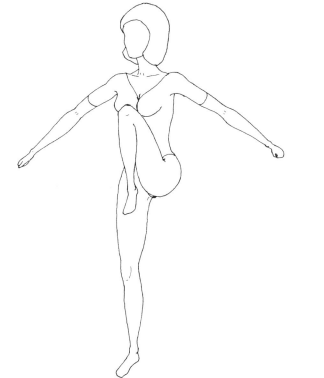

3 Using The Legs-Kicks

Women seldom have very strong arms and they are certainly no match for a man's, so, you have to compensate. Your legs can be very efficient weapons. In following the advice of the psychologist (if you are going to fight you have got to make it count), it is very important to make the most of what you have. Remember, if you can stun an attacker for just 10 or 20 seconds, then this gives you time to get help. It is advisable to practise the leg techniques we are about to show you as soon as you have warmed up. The more you practise, the better you will become. As the book progresses you will learn to strike an attacker as you effect your escape method. As your legs are much more powerful than your arms, it is obvious that your legs will be more effective in stunning an attacker than your arms.

We are going to explain only four basic kicks in this book; although there are many more, these four are enough for the time being. For purposes of simplicity, we are not going to ask you to learn the Japanese or Cantonese words for the various methods you are about to learn. Knowing what you are doing is all that is important. There are four basic kicks in this chapter which we call: a) front kick, b) side kick, c) roundhouse kick and d) back kick.

When practising the kicks, don't worry about trying to kick 3 feet above your head; it isn't necessary. It is far easier to kick an attacker's groin or stomach than his neck or head, although, with regular practice, there is no reason why you should not be able to kick as high as you want. The kicks have been practised for many years by martial arts practitioners in every part of the world. They have been proved effective time and time again and work with remarkable efficiency. Their only weakness is in their very effectiveness. Strike too hard and you will cause severe injury to the attacker, maybe even kill him.

It is a good idea to roll up an old carpet, tie it tightly into shape and use it for target practice. Hung from a tree or your garage roof, it will teach you how to control the power with which you kick. You see, even a rapist is protected by the Law. If you were to kill an attacker while trying to escape from him, you would probably have to answer a charge of manslaughter and that could prove very distressing. It would save a lot of problems if you were to break his leg or damage his groin. Then, if the attacker goes to hospital for treatment, he will have to explain the circumstances in which he received his injuries. In doing so, he would be admitting to his crime. Even if he lies about the circumstances, the police would be pretty quick in finding him. So do practise regularly, and do take care.

---

1. Front Kick

If you are standing with one leg in front of the other, then you can kick with either the leading leg or the rear leg.

If you look at Figure 1, you can see that the victim has her left leg in front of her right. Her arms and hands are held in front of her body as though she is cowering. In fact, they are held in front of her body for protection. But she wants the attacker to believe she is frightened and, because that is what he expects, that is how she is reacting. In doing this, she keeps surprise on her side.

Now look at Figure 2. The lady victim has raised her right (rear) leg up in front of her. Her knee is raised up to her chest. Her foot is kept tight to her body, close to her buttocks.

1

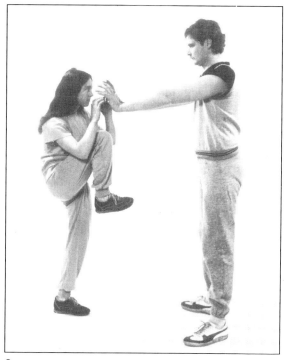

2

3

In Figure 3, she has kicked her leg out to the target. Her foot has travelled in a straight line from her buttocks to the target. She has struck the target with the ball of her foot because, if you strike with your toes while wearing soft shoes, the soles can easily bend downwards and injure you. So to prevent this, curl your toes towards your head and strike the target with the ball of your foot. Still looking at Figure 3, you can see that the lady victim is leaning slightly forward. This ensures that all of her body weight is going into the strike. You will also notice, in all three Figures, that at no time did her arms move. They remained in front of her body for protection from beginning to end.

Had our lady victim wanted to kick with her left (leading) leg, then she would have raised the left (leading) leg to her chest and kicked in the same way. She chose to kick with her right (rear) leg, because this has the added power of momentum. Immediately you have struck the target, retract your leg. If you leave it out, the attacker may grab it. Even if you miss the target, you must retract your leg immediately.

HOW TO PRACTISE

You must start slowly and gently. Begin by standing upright, holding your arms out to the sides at an angle of about 45° from your body. Then gently raise your knees up to your chest, alternating left and right. As you raise your knees, make sure your foot is tight into your body, close to your buttocks. Do this five or ten times with each leg. Then, standing in the same position, arms still outstretched, swing your leg up to waist height, keeping both of your legs straight, just as you did in the Warm Up earlier. Do this again about five or ten times with each leg. If your legs go higher than your waist that's fine. If they don't get as high as your waist, don't worry; it will not be long before they do. Now you can put the two movements together.

Still standing in the same position, with arms outstretched, raise one knee to your chest and then immediately thrust your raised leg forward, raise and strike. Repeat about five or ten times with each leg. When you have done that, go back to the sequence of Figures. Look at how our lady victim is standing. She gives the impression of being frightened. Look at her legs: her left (leading) leg is in front of the right (rear) leg. Her arms are in front of her upper body for protection. Figure 2 shows the lady with her right (rear) leg swung up to her chest and then, in Figure 3, she has thrust her raised leg in a straight line to the target. As she thrusts her leg, she also leans forward for maximum efficiency.

Now you try it. Start by striking firstly with the right (rear) leg and then with the left (leading) leg. Try five to ten kicks with each leg and then change around, so that you have your right leg in front and your left leg behind; then try another five or ten kicks with each leg.

We have asked you to practise this kick using two movements, i.e. raise and thrust, and this is quite correct, but now we are going to ask you to consider this. If you break the kick down into two movements, i.e. raise and thrust, would you agree that once you have raised your knee to your chest, there is a slight pause before you thrust? If so, you are not alone. It is the same for everyone at first. What you have to do is to make the kick into one flowing movement. The only way to ensure this is to practise, practise, practise. It won't be

long before you get it right. You see, in a real attack, if you pause before you strike with your knee raised, it is not going to be too difficult for the attacker to figure out what you are going to do next. Look at Figure 2 and you will understand what I mean. If you hold that position for too long, he'll know what's coming next and take evasive action to avoid the kick. So, when you are practising, don't pause, make it one movement.

Try putting two kicks together, e.g. from Figure 3 kick first with your right (rear) leg, then put it down in front of your left leg and kick with your left; you could carry on all day if you wanted to.

Make sure you thrust in a straight line, from your buttocks to the target, and lean forward as you thrust. Imagine you are taking a giant step into a swimming pool where your foot seems to carry on forever. The last point to remember is this: always strike beyond the target. If you kick to the stomach, aim for a spot 2 or 3 feet behind it. This will insure penetration of the target. No matter what part of the body you aim for, always aim to go through and beyond the target.

A very good method for increasing your speed is television. Wait for the commercial break, then, when the frame changes, *kick,* and then *kick* again at the next frame change, and so on. It's not advisable to kick at the television – it upsets the family! We advise waiting for the commercial break simply because there seem to be lots of frame changes in a very short time. It's very doubtful if you will be able to keep up with the frame changes, but don't worry; very few practitioners can, even the very advanced ones find it difficult. In a real attack, if you have been forced to use the front kick remember, don't stand and wait for your attacker. As soon as you have kicked, *run!* Get help, don't be brave. If the attacker is on the floor screaming, don't worry. Get help, look after yourself. Don't wait to see if you've hurt him, put as much distance between you and him in as short a time as is humanly possible. If you wait around for him to get up, he's going to want one of two things when he's on his feet. A doctor, or your blood. Don't give him a chance to get the latter.

SUMMARY

1. Raise the knee of the striking leg up to your chest.

2. Thrust the striking foot in a straight line to the target.

3. Strike the target with the ball of your foot.

4. Retract your leg as soon as you have completed the kick.

---

2. Roundhouse Kick

The Roundhouse Kick is favoured by many senior martial art practitioners for two main reasons: firstly its speed and secondly, its penetration power. This kick, as with all the others, must be practised by starting slowly and gently. This is how it is done.

Look firstly at Figure 4. The victim is once again standing as though cowering. Her left leg is in front of her right leg. As the attacker approaches her, she immediately starts her kick.

Look at Figure 5. She has raised her right (rear) leg behind her. Her leg is bent at the knee and her foot is tucked into her bottom. She is standing on the toes of

4

5

6

7

her left (leading) leg. Her hands are still held in front of her for protection.

Now look at Figure 6. She is still on her toes, but is now turning into the attacker; her knee is moving forward towards him and her hands are still in front of her.

If you look at Figure 7, you will see that the victim has delivered the kick into the attacker's ribs, by simply straightening her striking leg and using her instep to strike the target.

As with all kicks, you must retract your leg as soon as you have kicked; don't leave your leg out for the attacker to get hold of.

HOW TO PRACTISE

Start by standing as the victim does in Figure 4. You should have both feet planted firmly on the floor. Your body should be upright, hands in front of you for protection, your weight evenly distributed on both feet. Once you have assumed the correct stance you can begin to practise.

Your left leg is in front of your right. Now, instead of kicking, imagine you are going to use your knee to strike the target. You are going to strike with your right leg. Push your right (rear) leg through a full 180°, keeping your right (rear) leg bent, as though using your knee to strike. As you push off on your right (rear) leg, stand onto the toes of your left (leading) leg and stay there as you move through the 180° turn. By standing on your toes, you will turn much faster into the target. You will probably find that you are turning more than 180°. If you are, don't worry, that is supposed to happen. If you are pushing off as hard as you can, you may even turn a full circle. Again, don't worry; all it means is that you are doing it properly.

Try this exercise five or ten times on each leg. Make sure you keep your body upright from start to finish. Only the striking leg should be bent; the foot of the striking leg should be tight into your bottom. Your hands should be held in front of you all the time. The inside of the thigh of your striking leg should be parallel to the floor (see Figures 4 and 5) from start to finish. You should try to get your knee to waist height. When you have mastered this exercise, repeat it again, but this time picture an imaginary target in front of you.

Go through the exercise just as before but now, as your knee is pointing at the target, *straighten* your leg. Snap it out straight. You strike the target with your instep. Do this five or ten times with each leg.

Once you have reached the stage of practising the full kick, concentrate on making it one flowing movement from start to finish. Don't worry if you can't kick high – a roundhouse kick to the side of an attacker's knee can stop him from running after you – but when practising, try and kick at least to waist height. It won't be long before you find you are kicking higher and higher. If you look at Figure 7, you can see that the victim has kicked the attacker in the ribs and that is enough to knock the wind out of him. As with all strikes, aim to go through and beyond the target for maximum efficiency and penetration power.

When you find it starting to come easy, try putting two kicks together with the same leg. Practising in this manner will insure that you retract your leg as soon as you have kicked the target. Try kicking once at knee height and then once at waist height, making sure you fully retract your leg as soon as you've kicked. Once you find that you are getting the hang of it, trying kicking with alternate legs. Start with your left leg leading and kick with your right, followed immediately by a kick with your left leg.

This is how it is done. Start by standing as our victim in Figure 4 and kick with your right leg. Once you have kicked with your right, as in Figure 7, place your foot on the floor in front of you so that you are standing with your right leg leading and your left leg behind you. Now kick with your left leg.

In practising alternate kicking, left/right or right/left, you may find that you feel awkward or clumsy. Don't worry; everyone feels the same at first. You feel this way because you are changing your momentum. If you kick first with your right leg, then your body momentum is following an anti-clockwise path; as you stop to kick with your left leg, it moves the opposite way, in a clockwise path. The directions describe a shape similar to the letter 'S'.

The roundhouse kick gets its speed from the way you stand on the toes of your leading leg. Its power comes from the momentum of your body and the way you snap out your leg. It is a very fast, powerful and effective kick and used correctly, it can inflict serious injury to an attacker's body. If you have followed my advice and rolled up a carpet to practise on, you will soon realise just how effective the roundhouse kick can be.

Practise this kick as soon as you have warmed up. Every time you are going to practise, you must always practise the leg techniques and the more you practise, the better you will become. Now that you have been taught two different kicks, try combining them. Start with, say, the front kick and follow it immediately with the roundhouse kick. You will find that these two kicks flow very easily together. The advantage of putting these two kicks together is that one kick is a linear (straight line) movement and the other is a circular movement – front-roundhouse. Therefore, by using these two kicks together, if the first one misses its target, you will still have the element of surprise on your side as the second kick, being a circular movement, will catch the attacker off his guard, thus allowing you to escape.

Another advantage of putting these two kicks together is that it will assist you in improving your balance and co-ordination.

SUMMARY
1. Push off with your rear leg and stand onto the toes of your leading leg.
2. Turn into the target on the toes of your leading leg, making sure that the striking foot is tight into your bottom.
3. Point the knee of the striking leg at the target.
4. Straighten the striking leg into the target.
5. Strike the target with the instep of the striking leg.
6. Retract your leg as soon as you have completed the kick.

3. Step Through Side Kick
The step through side kick is thought of by many senior martial art practitioners as the *most* powerful of all kicks. Sometimes referred to as 'the cannon kick', it is, at the very least, devastating! Anyone who has had the misfortune to be hit with a step through side kick, will remember two things: firstly the pain and secondly the flying lesson! A great friend of mine (who is himself now a black-belt holder and instructor) often tells his students of the first time he tried to stop a step through side kick. He had at the time been a practitioner for about a year and was involved in a full contact school of martial art. These are his own words:

'I was at my class as usual on a Monday evening and was in combat with my instructor. My instructor was as usual letting me hit him, but I started getting a bit too cocky. My instructor decided that it was time for me to start calming down, I had made the fatal mistake of mistaking kindness for weakness. My instructor moved forward and by the time I saw his leg it was too late. Our gym was having the ceiling painted and about 15 feet behind me was a metal builders' frame going up to the ceiling. At first I thought I'd been split in half, then I hit the metal builders' frame. I was wrapped around it like a piece of forgotten spaghetti. I just

wanted to die: first of all there was the pain, and then that horrible feeling of uncontrolled flight as I flew backwards across the gym. I'm glad I hit the builders' frame, because if I hadn't, I probably would have gone right through the wall. Once I'd hit the frame I just sat on the floor, I didn't know what hit me, or where I was. I've never experienced anything like it, and I don't want to again either.'

8

Having read one person's account of what it feels like to be on the receiving end of a step through side kick, it must be pointed out that this gentleman had been in regular training for about a year when he experienced this kick. What is really frightening is what would the same kick have done to someone who was not in the same peak of condition? This is how it's done.

Look at Figure 8. The victim is again standing with her feet apart and her left leg is in front of her right. Her weight is evenly distributed between both feet and her hands are held in front of her body for protection (as though she is cowering).

Now look at Figure 9. Her right (rear) leg has moved forward behind her left (leading) leg. Look at Figure 9 closely. She has moved forward towards the attacker, crossing her legs with her hands still held in front of her body.

Look at Figure 10. She has raised her left (leading) leg and her knee is raised to her chest. The toes of her raised leg are pointing away from the attacker. Her supporting right leg is slightly bent to aid balance. Her hands are still in front of her body. Her body is upright.

Now look at Figure 11. The victim thrusts her raised leg at the attacker. She strikes the attacker with the base of her heel. Her striking heel moves in a straight line to the attacker's body. She is aiming to go through, and beyond the attacker's body.

As soon as you have kicked, retract your leg. You don't have to worry about kicking high at the moment; the more you practise the higher you'll kick. A step through side kick to an attacker's leg can easily break it, thus insuring that he can't chase you.

9

10

11

Start slowly and gently. Look at Figure 8. The victim is standing as usual. She looks frightened. Her left leg is in front of her right. From this position, break the kick down into three movements. Start by moving your right (rear) leg forward and behind your left (leading) leg, as in Figure 9. Try doing that five or six times with each side of your body, until you get the feel of the movement. Now add a little more.

Look at Figure 10. This time step behind your left (leading) leg and now raise your left (leading) leg so that your knee is up to your chest. Make sure that your foot is tucked tight into your bottom and that your toes are pointing away from the attacker. Try that five or six times on each side of your body, step through, raise your knee. Once you have the feel of it and it's coming easily, look at Figure 10.

Standing in this position, practise the actual strike. Making sure that your toes point away from the target and that your striking foot travels in a straight line, strike the target with the flat of your heel for maximum efficiency. Do that five or six times on each leg, then go through the whole combination of movements. Step through, raise your knee and strike.

Have all the figures in front of you when you practise. Try and make the combination of movements flow as though they were only one movement. Practise the step through side kick every time you practise, preferably as soon as you have warmed up.

Once you have the hang of the step through side kick in the way I have explained, you can increase your speed a great deal in the following way: instead of stepping behind your leading leg, try hopping behind it, then raise your knee and strike as you just have.

You have now been taught three different methods of kicking. Your arsenal of physical weapons is already starting to build up. If you have not yet followed my advice and rolled up an old carpet to practise on, then you'd better do it right now! The leg techniques I have already taught you must be used with *control*. You must learn to exercise *control* when kicking. Strike too hard and you are going to maim the person you are kicking!

Now that you know three methods of kicking, try putting them together in combination. You can put them together in any order you like. They will, with a little practise, flow from one to the other. Try putting these combinations together:

1. Front kick, roundhouse kick and step through side kick.
2. Step through side kick, front kick and roundhouse kick.
3. Roundhouse kick, step through side kick and front kick.

Make up your own combinations; it's up to you. You must decide for yourself what works for you. If you are faced with an attacker, you are not going to have time to practise first, you are going to have to get on with it by yourself. It's your choice, so make sure you make it count!

SUMMARY
1. Move your rear leg forward by stepping behind the leading leg.
2. Raise the striking (leading) leg so that your knee is up to your chest. Make sure that the striking foot is tucked tight into your bottom and that the toes of the striking foot are pointing away from the target.
3. Straighten the striking leg into the target.
4. Strike the target with the flat of your heel.
5. Retract your leg as soon as you have completed the kick.

4. Back Kick

The back kick is a superb method of kicking and is not, as it may sound a way of kicking backwards. It is usually a follow-up kick, but it can be used as a first kick. (You will understand that sentence better once you start to practise).

Look at Figure 12. The victim is standing in the usual way, hands in front of her body for protection, as though cowering. Her left leg is in front of her right, her body is upright, her weight is evenly distributed on both feet.

Now look at Figure 13. The victim has started to move her body in a clockwise movement.

In Figure 14 she has completely turned her back to the attacker. You will notice that the victim's feet, though turning, remained on the same spots throughout the turn. You will understand this point more fully when you read the practice pages for this kick.

Now look at Figure 15. The victim has raised her right knee up to her chest, her right foot is tucked in tight to her bottom; her toes are pointing away from the attacker.

In Figure 16, the victim has thrust her raised leg in a straight line to the attacker's body. She strikes the target with the flat of her heel for maximum efficiency. The toes of her striking foot are pointing to the floor to ensure that she strikes with her heel.

It may sound complicated, but I promise you it isn't. You have already managed three kicks and this is the last one. Let's move straight on to the practice; then you'll know how easy and straightforward it really is.

HOW TO PRACTISE
Look at Figure 12. From this position we are going to break down the kick into three movements. Figure 12 shows the victim in the usual position; her left leg is in front of her right. Now look at Figure 13, particularly the position of her feet. She has started to turn in a clockwise movement and, although her feet are turning, they remain on the same spot on the floor. You can see in Figures 12 and 13 that her left leg is closest to the attacker, even though she is turning her body. Now look

12

at Figure 14. Look closely at the victim's feet: although she has completely turned her back on the attacker, her left leg is still closest to the attacker. The heels of both feet are pointing towards the attacker and she has turned on the balls of her feet for speed. Still looking at Figure 15: the victim's back is towards the attacker and she is looking over her right shoulder at the attacker.

This is the first movement. Try it yourself a few times. Have Figures 13, 14 and 15 in front of you and practise the turn., Start with your left leg in front of the right and turn on the balls of your feet in a clockwise motion, making sure your feet stay on the same spots as you turn your back to the attacker. Try this five or six times. Then try it with your right leg in front of your

13

14

15

16

left: from this position you will turn in an anti-clockwise motion and look over your left shoulder at the attacker. Once you have the hang of the turn, the rest is easy.

Now we will add a little more. Starting with your left leg leading, as in Figure 12, go through the clockwise turn as you have already practised so that you are standing in the same way as the victim in Figure 14. From this position, raise your right leg so that your knee is up to your chest and your foot is tight into your bottom, as in Figure 15. When you have practised the turn several times and have it right, try the turn and add the leg raise as I've just explained. When you have that right and are looking over the correct shoulder at the attacker, all you have to do is add the strike.

Look at Figure 15. The victim's toes are pointing away from the attacker as he approaches her. From this position, she thrusts her foot out at the attacker's body (Figure 16) and strikes the target with the flat of her heel. As with any strike, she aims to go through and beyond the target. Now that you have practised the kick a piece at a time, try the whole combination, but practise it slowly and gently. Once you begin to find it coming easy you can start to increase your speed. Here are a few ways of making it faster:

Assuming that you are starting with your left leg leading and turning in a clockwise motion, try raising your striking (right) leg as you turn. This will improve your speed very considerably because, once you have completed your turn, your striking leg will be ready to strike. Another tip for increasing your speed, still assuming that you are starting with your left leg leading, is to throw your arms in a clockwise motion behind you as you turn. This not only increases the speed of your turn, but also increases the power in your strike because of the added momentum. A final tip (you still have your left leg leading), spin your head in a clockwise motion as fast as you can, all the way round, a full 360°, so that you are facing the attacker almost immediately. This will increase your speed simply because, as soon as you can see the attacker, you can let the kick go!

There are several important points to remember when using the back kick. Firstly you must turn *fast*. If you turn too slowly you will have your back to the attacker for too long and this may give him a chance to move

away from your kick. If you remember this simple rule then you won't turn slowly: when using the back kick, the first thing to hit the target is *your eyes!* Remember that rule when practising the back kick and you should overcome the danger of turning too slowly. Another point to consider is the force you strike with. The back kick is often considered just as devastating as the step through side kick and you have already heard one account of how it feels to be on the receiving end of that! When practising the back kick, don't overdo it. If you start feeling dizzy or sick, then stop. When you strike, make sure you do so with the flat of your heel for maximum efficiency. Your foot should travel in a straight line to the target and, as with all the kicks, retract your leg as soon as you have kicked; don't leave it out for the attacker to grab!

Now I will move onto the back kick in its true sense: kicking backwards. This method of kicking is very easy indeed. Assuming that you are standing with your right leg leading and the attacker approaches you from behind, simply raise your right leg (as in Figure 15) and thrust backwards to the target (as in Figure 16). It is that simple. You may find that you prefer to kick with the left leg. That's fine. Whatever suits your body best is obviously what is best for you.

Whether you have to use the back kick to kick backwards or forwards don't worry if you can't kick high. A back kick to an attacker's knee or thigh can cause him serious injury; it could even break his leg. You don't have to kick high to be effective. In fact, I shall advise you later to use a backwards back kick to an attacker's feet or shins in order to escape from an attack from the rear.

You must practise the back kick every time you practise your escape methods. As with all the kicks, practise every time after you warm up.

SUMMARY
1. Spin your body so that your back is to the target and, as you spin raise your rear leg so that your knee is raised up to your chest. Make sure that your toes are pointing away from the target.

2. Look over the shoulder of the raised leg (i.e. if the right leg is raised look over the right shoulder and *vice versa*).

3. Thrust the striking (raised) leg into the target. The striking leg moves in a straight line to the target.

4. Strike the target with the flat of your heel making sure that your toes are pointing to the floor on impact.

5. Retract your leg as soon as you have completed the kick.

CONCLUSION

I have described four basic kicks in this chapter, but don't let the term 'basic kicks' worry you. The average man in the street knows only one way to kick – badly. He certainly doesn't know how to avoid any of the kicks which I have taught you but, more importantly, he doesn't expect *you* to know how to kick properly. Surprise is what shocks and stuns a would-be attacker. Put yourself in the attacker's shoes. Would you expect your female victim to be able to kick in four different ways? Would you expect your female victim to turn her back on you and then deliver a kick (the back kick) like a mule? Would you expect your female victim to half turn her body and deliver a kick (the roundhouse kick) hard enough to break your ribs or knee? Would you expect your female victim to take what looks like a step forward, and then kick (the step through side kick) so hard that you feel as though you've been split in half?

Think about it? Would you expect any of those things to happen? I doubt it. You see, what makes these kicks so effective is that, when you are on the receiving end, you can't see them coming until it is too late. The only people who might recognise what you are doing are martial art practitioners and the chances of being attacked by a practitioner are millions and millions to one against.

The kicks I have taught you, once perfected, can inflict serious injury, possibly even death to anyone being hit by them, so practise *control* on a rolled-up carpet, as I described earlier. They are designed to flow, one into the other, and can be practised in any

order and put together in any combination you like. A great favourite of most newcomers to self defence martial art is the roundhouse/back kick combination. Suppose you start with your left leg leading; you would firstly use a roundhouse kick with your right leg, place your right leg down in front of your left leg after striking, then, using your body's momentum, go immediately into your back kick, kicking with your left leg. This combination is normally used if the first (roundhouse) kick misses the target. Because your momentum is carrying you in an anti-clockwise direction, the back kick flows very quickly and naturally as a follow-up kick.

Try this combination for yourself. If you like it and it works for you, then practise it as often as you can. The more you practise, the more effective you will become. It is much better, though, to find your own combinations, because what works for one, may not work for another. *You* must decide for yourself what complements your body best. In a real attack, it is *you* who decides what to do. Whether you escape using a single strike or a combination of strikes is not important; what *is* important is that you *do* escape, using the methods that work best for you.

I have already explained how much injury you can inflict using these kicks and I must point out that it is *not* my intention that a woman being attacked should seriously injure, maim or kill an attacker. It *is* my intention that any woman being attacked should know how to escape. *Do not* use these kicks unless there is absolutely *no* other way possible to escape. If in any doubt whatsoever, *don't use them.*

4 Running Escapes

A common reaction to danger of any kind is to want to get away from it. This is one of the many similarities we encountered during our research. It's common sense isn't it? But the manner in which one tries to escape the danger differs slightly from case to case. Some of the people we interviewed told us that they just curled up into a ball on the floor, protecting their heads. Others told us that they ran as fast as they could. Some others just froze and were too afraid to do anything at all. Well let's have a look at all three things:

1. Those who curled up in a ball on the floor. If you are on the floor, you can still be kicked and punched. If an attacker picks up a brick, or something else with which he can hit you, it doesn't seem very sensible at all.

2. Those who ran as fast as they could. Again, this seems sensible. But, if you can run, it's fairly safe to assume that your attacker can also run. You still have to escape the danger not have it 3 or 4 feet behind you.

3. Those who just froze. Sadly, there's not very much I can say, except that those women who froze were raped or sexually assaulted.

Unfortunate though it is, you must be prepared to help yourself. Freeze and you'll become one of the statistics you have already read about. Curl up in a ball and you will probably give up in the end anyway and you too will become another statistic. Run as fast as you can and at least you're doing something positive to escape the danger, even though the danger is still just a few feet behind you. So let's have a look at this manner of escape *running*.

Firstly, it's no good running blindly. If you do, you may run into a blind alley and then you will be trapped. You have to run to safety: you have to get help. You may decide, if it is late at night, to run into a pub or a garage, which is fine. In the case of a very serious attack, you may not be fortunate enough to be near either of those places, so you could run to a front door, banging as hard as you can. It may well confuse the occupants, but it will help to get you out of trouble. No matter where you decide to run, one thing is certain: if the attacker wants you badly enough, he is going to run after you and even if your destination is only 200 yards or so away, it is going to seem more like 200 miles. You are going to want more time, say 10 or 20 seconds. How then can you get this extra time? Well, you could hide, but you first have to make certain that the attacker doesn't see the place you have chosen, and that's not easy when he's only a few feet behind you. You have got to stop him from chasing you somehow. Here's one method you can use. I discovered this method in the back streets of Liverpool when I was a very young child. It rescued me from trouble countless times.

Running Escape

You are running as fast as you can and the attacker is catching you up fast; when he is about 2 or 3 feet behind you, *stop*, and immediately kneel down on the floor. Because he is not expecting it, your body will act as a trip wire and over he will go. I needn't tell you how much damage this could do if there was some kind of obstacle, say a lamp post, in front of you when he goes over you head first. This method of escape can cause serious injury to an attacker. It's up to you whether or not to go down in front of an obstacle but your action will at the very least trip him up and normally put him on the floor, giving you those precious seconds you need to escape. There are some important points to remember when applying this method of escape, so we will move straight on to the best way to practise.

HOW TO PRACTISE

Look firstly at Figures 17 and 18. These two figures show the victim in the kneeling position. Figure 17 shows the victim from the left side of her body. Look carefully at the position of her legs. Her left foot is planted firmly on the floor and her left knee is supporting her body. Look now at Figure 18. Her right knee is on the floor. In both Figures, you can see that her head is tucked well down and her arms are perfectly straight, locked at the elbows. Her body position may remind you of an athlete about to start a race and you would be quite right in assuming this because, as soon as the attacker has gone over the top of his victim, she is not going to wait for him to get up. She is going to run as fast as she can to get help.

Figures 19 and 20 show the effect this escape method has on the unsuspecting attacker. When effecting this escape method it is most important to make sure your head is tucked well down. If it isn't, then you may well be struck by the attacker's knees as he sails over you.

Once the attacker has gone over the top of you, he will be on the floor in front of you so, when you *run*, don't run towards him. Run away from him in the opposite direction. If he has injured himself, he will probably give up the chase.

17

18

19

20

21

22

The way to master this technique is the same as for any other method. Start slowly and gently. Begin by walking just a few paces and gently kneel to the floor, making sure you have adopted the correct position. When you have it right, try jogging for a few paces and then stop and kneel. Once you have it right when jogging, then you can try running and stopping. It doesn't take long to perfect this method of escape and, once mastered, may well save you a lot of trouble.

There is one slight danger in this method: you may stop too soon, too far in front of the attacker, or the attacker may have very fast reflexes. In either case, you are going to be in a very dangerous situation as you are going to be kneeling on the floor with the attacker standing behind you. Now you must act fast and this is what to do. Look at Figure 21. Our lady victim has raised her knee up to her chest and, at the same time, has straightened the other leg. Look now at Figure 22. The lady victim has thrusted her leg backwards, just as you did in the back kick earlier. She strikes the target with the heel for maximum efficiency. As soon as she has struck the target, she runs. Now we have used what seemed a dangerous situation to our advantage, but you must be quick to make it count. *Hit* and *run*. Don't look back; don't stop until you reach help.

SUMMARY

1. Check the distance between you and the attacker before you take any action.

2. When the attacker is approximately 2 to 3 feet behind you *stop* and kneel. Make sure that you are in the correct kneeling position.

3. If the attacker trips over your body; *run* in the opposite direction, *away* from the attacker.

4. If the attacker does not trip over your body; raise the knee that is on the floor up to your chest.

5. Extend the raised leg in a straight line into the target.

6. Strike the target with the flat of your heel.

7. Retract your leg as soon as you have completed the kick.

8. Run away from the attacker as fast as you can. You should be running in the direction you are facing.

CONCLUSION

Escape from an attacker while he is running after you and you can gain those vital seconds you need to get help. It is an important point to remember that the attacker is *not* expecting you to put him on the floor whilst he is running after you. When used correctly, this escape method can be enough to deter an attacker from bothering you any further, but it is never safe to assume that you have completely escaped. So don't put yourself into a false sense of security. Once he's down, keep running and get help. Even if you haven't been injured, you could still be at risk. Don't take any chances, get away!

5 Walking Escapes

Now that you know how to escape while being chased and how to kick so it counts, it is time to move on. You must always remember how to escape if being chased because, from now on, every time we show you a method of escape, we shall tell you not to be brave but to *run*.

One of the most common attackers of women is the late-night drunk. He is generally more of a nuisance than a danger and normally a few stern words are enough to deter his advances. However, even this type of attack can turn nasty. It usually starts with him trying to chat you up. You know the type of thing: 'Hello darling, you going my way? Can I take you home?' At this stage it's just a nuisance, but if he's feeling a little adventurous he may put his arm around you. Still a nuisance; even though you have told him to stop, he persists. Then it happens! His arm is around your shoulder and his hand wanders onto your breast. At this point you are being sexually assaulted. You must act quickly and firmly; don't let it go any further.

You could start shouting and screaming at him. In fact, this will often be enough to stop him, especially if the assault is happening in a crowded street. He'll probably apologise for fear of being caught. He will probably tell you it was an accident and that it was unintentional and, if he does, that's fine. Your pride will be hurt, and you will probably feel pretty shaken up, but at least you've suffered no physical injury and that's at least some consolation.

On the other hand, this attack can and does, happen in less crowded areas where there is no one to help you. In this case, he doesn't have to apologise to you; he can carry on with the assault. Now we have a serious danger to contend with and, as far as we know, there's nobody at hand to help – just you and the attacker. So for this very situation, I am going to show you various methods of escape.

Walking Escape No.1

Figure 23 shows our lady victim in the situation we have just described. She has told the man several times to *stop* and she has even walked away from him, but now he's caught up with her and he's started to molest her again. Now she is really worried. She knows she must act quickly to get away. Look again at Figure 23, the attacker's left arm is around the victim's shoulder. She has taken hold of his left wrist with her left hand.

Now look at Figure 24. The victim has simply dropped her head, as though looking to the floor, and her body is upright. As she dropped her head, she took the attacker's left arm over her own head, turning his wrist clockwise, so that the palm of his hand was facing her as in Figure 25. Once his left arm has been taken over her head, level with her mouth and with the palm of his hand towards her, she places her right hand onto his left elbow, as in Figure 25. (You will notice that at no time has her body dropped.) She now pulls his left hand towards her left shoulder and, at the same time, she leans her right shoulder forward, so that all of her weight leans into his left elbow.

Now look at Figure 26 and you can see the outcome of this combination of movements. The attacker is now prone and completely at the victim's mercy.

Now that you have the attacker in a prone position, it is up to you what to do next. If you lean forward from the waist, you could put him completely onto the floor. On the other hand, you could tell him not to do it again and let him go? Or, you could look very carefully at Figure 26. Up to now you have hurt nothing more than his pride but Figure 26 will show you some very interesting targets. The right side of his body is completely open to a knee attack. His head is about 2 feet away from the victim's left foot. His legs are very wide apart, offering his masculinity. His left foot is in a

23

24

25

26

prime position for breaking, as is his left knee. Had you applied all of your weight to his elbow (by leaning forward from the waist), the attacker would have ended up face down on the floor. The target area then would have been the back of his entire body. In that case, simply stamping down as hard as you can with your heel onto one of his legs would cause him severe distress. It would certainly have stopped him running after you.

It is not for me to condone injuring an attacker and I certainly never condone violence of any kind. It is for you to decide what to do if faced with this situation. I have simply pointed out the possibilities open to you. You must decide for yourself what is the safest thing to do in these circumstances. Whatever you decide, it is *you* that ultimately faces the consequences for *your* actions. If you don't stop the attacker, then he will more than likely come after you again, perhaps even want to cause you some serious injury. If you do stop him by injuring him, it is you that will have to go to Court. No matter what you do, you are taking a risk.

HOW TO PRACTISE

This escape works best when you are moving forward, as would happen in a real attack but first, practise with a partner while standing still. This will help you get it right and, at the same time, you will discover that it also works well without moving (just right for the office wolf).

The important points to remember are these: when you take the attacker's arm over your head, make sure you only drop your head as though looking to the floor. Keep your body upright. If attacked by the attacker's left arm, make certain you turn his wrist clockwise as you take his arm over your head. This will ensure that his elbow is in the correct position to carry out your escape. If attacked by the attacker's right arm, then you should turn it anti-clockwise for the same reason.

Once his arm is over your head, keep it level with your mouth; this will enable you to see with ease where his elbow is situated. When you apply your right arm to his elbow, make sure you keep his left hand close to your right shoulder. This is important for the leverage. Lastly, make absolutely certain that, when you push on his elbow, you also pull on his hand, making sure that

you push forward and down at an angle of roughly 45°.

When you have practised this a few times and find that it is starting to work quite easily, start practising while you are walking forward. You will find it even easier, because you will have the added advantage of momentum on your side.

SUMMARY
This summary assumes the attacker is standing to the right of the victim, using his left arm for the attack.
1. Take the attacker's left wrist in your left hand.
2. Keep hold of the attacker's wrist and drop your head as though looking to the floor. Keep your body upright.
3. Take the attacker's arm over the top of your head and twist his wrist clockwise so that the palm of his hand is facing you. Keep your body upright.
4. With the attacker's arm held in front of your mouth, place your right hand on his elbow.
5. Pull his wrist into your left shoulder and push forward and down with your right hand. Lean forward as you push his elbow with your right hand. Keep his left hand close to your left shoulder as you push against his elbow with your right hand.
6. The attacker will be forced down in an arm lock. Once you have forced him down the rest is up to you.

Walking Escape No.2
Once you have the first escape method, you may be wondering how else you could escape from this situation? Well, that depends on how much damage you want to do to the attacker. If you were to feel really threatened, then you may think it safer to stun and shock an attacker before escaping. Here is one way to really knock the wind out of his sails.

Look at Figure 27. The victim has been attacked in the same way as before, but this time she has taken hold of the attacker's left wrist and pulled it down hard. At the same time, she arches her neck backwards. This locks the attacker's (left) arm around her shoulder. Also, the victim has taken her *right* arm across her body and you can see that the attacker's body is wide open to attack.

27

Now look at Figure 28. The victim has snapped her right elbow back across her body, straight into the attacker's solar plexus. She strikes the target as hard as she possibly can. She strikes as usual, aiming to go through and beyond the target. She strikes to the attacker's solar plexus because she wants to wind him. She could have aimed her elbow at his head, but this could have injured him seriously. The solar plexus or stomach are the best targets to aim for. Striking either of these targets in the manner explained, will cause the attacker considerable distress.

Once you have struck the attacker you can carry on escaping as you did previously, or just run away.

HOW TO PRACTISE

This escape method is the same as the first one. First of all, practise it while standing still until you get the feel of it. Then try it while walking. These are the important things to concentrate on. Firstly, make sure you grip the attacker's wrist firmly. Make certain that, as you pull it down, you arch your head backwards; this will ensure that his arm is locked around your shoulder as in Figure 27. You must take your striking (right) arm all the way across your body before you strike! When you strike, make sure your arm is bent so that you strike with the elbow. If practising with a friend, *don't* make contact with your elbow; if you do, you'll lose a friend. Concentrate on the target area. The target area is just below the attacker's sternum (breast bone) where there is no bone. *Be careful* not to make contact – it is very dangerous! Practise on your rolled-up carpet and you will soon realise how powerful the elbow strike really is. This striking method is very fast and will take the attacker completely by surprise. If you use it, don't wait to see how much damage you've done. *Run* and get help!

Many of the women who come to our classes like this escape method very much and, instead of striking only once to the attacker's solar plexus or stomach, they like to strike two, or even three, times. The first strike is usually to the attacker's solar plexus or stomach and the second strike is usually to the attacker's head (face). Those women who like to strike three times aim the third strike to the attacker's groin. They do this by simply bending their knees and striking in the same way.

SUMMARY

N.B. This summary assumes that the attacker is standing to the right of the victim and uses his left arm for the attack.

1. Take hold of the attacker's left wrist with your left hand.

2. Arch your neck backwards and pull down hard with your left hand.

3. Take your right arm across your body as far as you can.

4. Snap your right arm back across your body as fast as you can. Bend your arm at the elbow as you snap it across.

5. Strike the target with your elbow as hard as you can.

6. If you wish to strike the target more than once; follow steps 3, 4 and 5 again.

7. If you do not wish to strike the target more than once, *run*.

Walking Escape No.3

It is possible to break an attacker's leg if attacked in this way. I am going to show you how it is done simply because I believe that you should have alternative methods of escape from each type of attack. It is up to you to decide which escape method works best for *you*. This is how its done:

Look at Figure 29. From the same attack, the victim has stepped forward and to her left. (She probably used an elbow strike first.)

Now look at Figure 30. She has taken the attacker's left arm over her head (as you did earlier) and is holding his left wrist with both her hands. She has raised her right knee in readiness for a side kick.

In Figure 31, she has pulled the attacker's arm towards her; this is done to make sure the attacker's weight is on his left leg. As she pulls him forward, she also strikes with a side kick to the attacker's knee. She strikes with the flat of her heel for maximum efficiency. Once she has kicked, she *runs* to get help. She doesn't wait to see how much damage she's done.

29

30

31

HOW TO PRACTISE

It's best to practise this escape while walking forward. Start slowly and gently. As you are walking slowly forward with the attacker's left arm around your shoulder, step to *your* left. Make sure you have a tight grip on his wrist as you step to the left. As you are stepping to the left, take his left arm over your head, just as you did before. Once his left arm is in front of you get a tight grip on it with both hands as in Figure 30. Now pull his arm towards you as you raise your knee for the side kick. At this stage, the attacker may well pull back and, if he does, it is going to make it even worse for him, because, in pulling back, he is going to add to the power of your side kick. As you pull him towards you let the side kick go!

Aim straight for his knee as in Figure 31. Pull yourself into the kick and make sure you strike with the flat of your heel. If you are practising with a friend, take it easy. *Do not* make contact with your kick. You'll break your friend's leg! When practising this escape method, have Figures 29 to 31 in front of you. Practise being attacked from both sides of your body. Obviously, if you are attacked from the other side of your body, you will step to your right and kick with your left.

SUMMARY

N.B. This summary assumes that the attacker is standing to the right of the victim and uses his left arm for the attack.

1. Take the attacker's left wrist in your left hand.

2. Drop your head as though looking to the floor.

3. Take the attacker's wrist over your head and step to your left as you take his arm over.

4. As you take his arm over your head, grip his left wrist with your right hand so that you are now holding it with both of your hands.

5. *Stop* and raise your right knee up to your chest in preparation for a side kick. Keep hold of his wrist with both hands.

6. Pull the attacker's arm towards you and strike with a side kick to the side of his knee.

7. As soon as you have completed the kick retract your leg.

8. *Run!*

CONCLUSION

I have described three different ways to escape from this type of attack and each one, used correctly, will get you out of trouble. It is up to you to decide which method will work best for *you*. You can mix all three methods together if you like. For instance, you may decide it is a good idea to stun the attacker with an elbow strike and then put him on the floor, as you did in the first escape. Alternatively, you may decide to stun him with an elbow strike and break his leg as well. You know how to do it; it's up to you.

I believe that it is always best to try and talk your way out of a situation or, better still, avoid it.

The weakness of these escape methods is in their very effectiveness. Use them only when it is absolutely necessary and if there is no other possible way to escape. They don't take long to learn, but, once used, it will take a long time for their effects to be overcome.

6 Free Standing Holds-Strangles

In this and the next three chapters, on free standing holds, we shall deal with the many various ways women are held in attack situations. We shall cover the milder nuisance type of attack and go right through to the more serious violent type attack. I shall show you how you can expect to be held by an attacker and, of course, how to escape from this hold. This section is the most favoured by the women who attend our classes, because we are really getting down to the business of self defence. We shall be using both hard and soft styles to escape the various holds. Once again, it will be up to you how to escape. Whether you use a hard or soft style to escape is *your* choice.

During our research, we found many similarities in attack situations. For instance, in a serious attack situation, a man would usually hold his victim with one hand and try to remove her clothing with the other. We have exploited this similarity to the full. It is a weakness on the part of the attacker because it is much easier to escape if you are held with one hand than with two. It makes sense, doesn't it?

We shall also show you how to escape from an attacker who holds you with two hands. Another similarity which we have fully exploited is that an attacker who holds you with both hands normally holds you so that his arms are trapping yours against your body. This is another weakness on the part of the attacker because, when he holds you with both his arms, he is concentrating on keeping your arms still and therefore doesn't know what your hands, knees and feet are doing. All the similarities we discovered have been fully exploited to work against the attacker, but I will explain them in more detail as we progress through this section.

Let us start with the stranglehold which, in itself, is not very difficult to escape from. As long as you can distinguish the difference between a straight arm strangle and a bent arm strangle, it is fairly simple to escape from either. Look at Figures 32 and 33. Figure 32 shows the straight arm strangle and 33 the bent arm strangle. Apart from the obvious differences between straight and bent arms, you can also see that there is a pronounced difference in the distance between attacker and victim.

In Figure 32, the straight arm strangle, you can see that there is quite a lot of distance between attacker and victim, while in Figure 33, the bent arm strangle, there is hardly any distance at all. Looking at both Figures, you don't have to be a genius to work out that both the victim's arms and hands are free to employ the escape method of her choice.

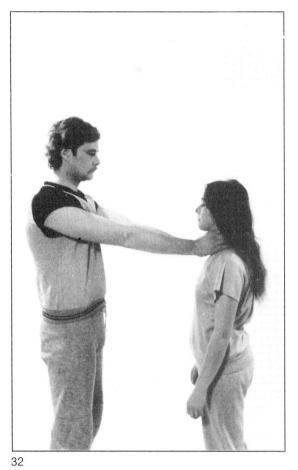

32

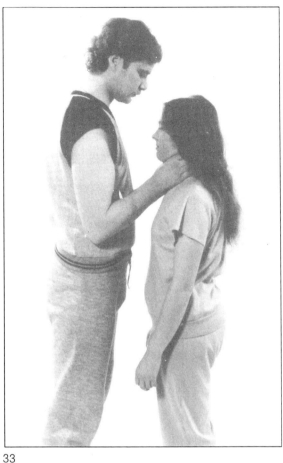

33

STRAIGHT ARM STRANGLE

Let's deal first with the straight arm strangle. Figure 32 shows this type of attack. The escapes you can employ are countless. Let us keep it gentle to start with.

Straight Arm Strangle Escape No.1

Look at Figure 34. The victim has gripped the attacker's little fingers on both of his hands and is bending them backwards against the joints. Look closely at the position of the victim's fingers and thumbs. Her thumbs are held into the attacker's knuckles of his little fingers and her fingers are at the tips of the attacker's little fingers. This ensures that she applies maximum leverage to his joints.

Now look at Figure 35. The victim has applied pressure to the attacker's fingers and he has released his hold. She is keeping his hands close to her body and is forcing the attacker's hands downwards.

Now look at Figure 36. She has forced the attacker completely to the floor. Now it is up to her what happens next. As you can see, the attacker's head is wide

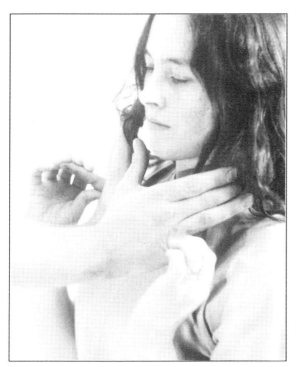

34

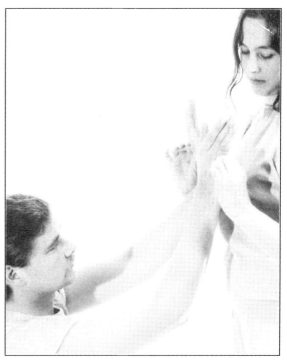

35

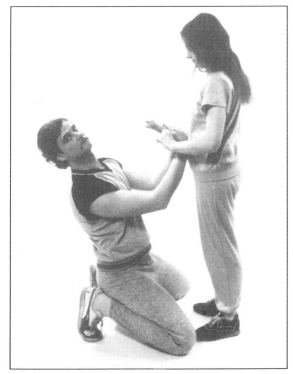

36

37

open to a knee strike and his body to a front kick. It's her choice.

In Figure 37, the victim has applied her hands to the attacker's little fingers but has also used a front kick to his groin. The front kick can be used at any time during this attack. If she kicks him first, it will weaken his grip considerably.

HOW TO PRACTISE

You must practise gripping your partner's little fingers. Make sure you bend both of his fingers backwards at the same time. Keep his hands close to your body as you bend his fingers backwards. This will force him to the floor. If you are practising with a friend be careful. If you bend the little fingers back too quickly you will very likely break them. Take it easy when you practise.

SUMMARY

1. Place your thumbs onto the knuckles of your attacker's little fingers.

2. Place your fingers at the tips (the fingerprint side) of his little fingers.

3. Bend his little fingers backwards with both of your hands.

4. As you bend his little fingers backwards, keep his hands close to your body and force his hands downwards.

5. Your attacker will be forced to go down in front of you. The hold has been released so it is up to you to decide whether any further action is necessary.

6. *Run.*

Straight Arm Strangle Escape No.2

Another simple method to escape from the straight arm strangle is to break the attacker's grip using your arms and body weight. Look at Figure 38. The victim has thrown her right arm into the air. Her arm is straight.

Now look at Figure 39. She has thrown her arm in a full circle over the top of the attacker's arms. The attacker's arms are now trapped by the victim's right arm. As the victim threw her right arm over the top of the attacker's arms, she also twisted her body in an anti-clockwise direction. This twisting motion made full use of her body weight to trap the attacker's arms. Still looking at Figure 39, you can see that the victim's left hand is wrapped around her right fist. Look at the position of the attacker's head in relation to the victim's right arm. Can you guess what she is going to do next?

Look at Figure 40. She strikes backwards into the attacker's head/face with her elbow. (Just as you did in Chapter 3.) Then she runs to get help. She doesn't wait to see how much damage she's done. She gets away.

HOW TO PRACTISE

Assuming that you use your right arm to escape, start by clenching your right fist. At the same time, tighten the muscles in your right forearm. Now, with the muscles of your right arm completely tensed, throw it over the attacker's arms in a windmill fashion, keep your right arm straight as you do so. As your right arm goes over the attacker's arms, twist your body in an anti-clockwise direction. Your right arm and body move at the same time. Your right arm moves in a full circle. Practise that movement first. When you are getting it right, the attacker's arms should be trapped beneath your right armpit, as in Figure 39. You should catch your right fist with your left hand. When you have that part correct you can add the final movement.

Look at Figure 40. From this position, you simply wind your body back in a clockwise motion as fast as you can and strike your target with your right elbow *en route*. As you wind back to strike the target, push your right fist with your left hand for added power and make sure

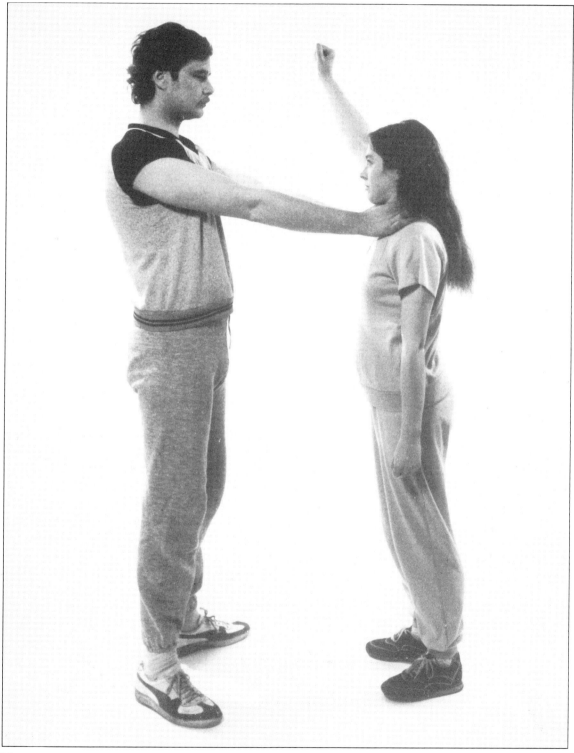

39

40

your arm is fully bent as you strike into your target. This will ensure that you strike the target with your elbow. When you practise with a friend, don't get over-enthusiastic, especially as you wind back to strike the target. Practise this part *very slowly*. *Do not* make contact.

SUMMARY

1. Clench your right fist and tense your right arm.

2. Two movements: throw your right arm in a full circle over both the attacker's arms; as you throw your arm over the attacker's arm, twist your body in an anti-clockwise direction.

3. Your right arm will now have the attacker's arms trapped beneath your right armpit. Cup your right fist with your left hand.

4. Two movements: strike back to the attacker's head with your right elbow; push your right fist with your left hand and twist your body clockwise as you strike.

5. *Run.*

Straight Arm Strangle Escape No. 3

The next method I shall describe of escaping from the straight arm strangle is a pure escape. If using this method, it is up to you to decide whether or not to use a strike to the attacker's body before or after you have escaped. This is how it is done.

Look at Figure 32. You can see that the victim's left arm is by her side. Now go on to look at Figures 41 and 42. The victim has taken her left arm over the top of the attacker's right arm and underneath his left elbow. Figure 42 shows the correct position in which the victim's left hand should be placed on the attacker's left elbow. It also shows the correct position of her right hand. Her right hand is holding her left hand. You can see that the victim has bent her knees slightly. This is to make ready for the next movement.

Now look at Figure 43. The victim has pushed her left hand in a circular motion with her right hand. She has straightened her legs to increase her power. She is leaning her torso slightly to her left. This allows her to

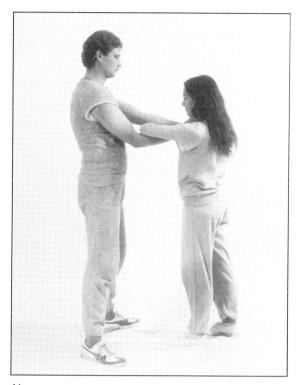

41

42

43

use her body weight. Both of her hands are pushing upwards against the attacker's left elbow. Her left elbow is on top of the attacker's right elbow. Because she has her left elbow on top of the attacker's right elbow as she pushes upwards with her hands, this has the effect of pushing downwards on the attacker's right elbow. The result is two movements in one. An upward and downward movement combined.

This may sound very complicated, but it isn't in fact. Let's go straight on to practising it and you will see just how simple it is.

HOW TO PRACTISE

Your left arm is going to move in a letter 'S' motion over the top of the attacker's right arm and underneath his left. Try that a few times – over his right and under his left.

Once you are used to the 'S' motion, concentrate on making sure that your left elbow is resting on top of his right elbow and that your left hand is underneath his left elbow. Try that a few times until you get it right. When you are getting it right, concentrate on your hands.

Your left hand should be underneath his left elbow, held tightly with your right hand as shown in Figure 42. Now go through it again but this time, as your arm travels in the 'S' motion, bend your knees slightly as in Figure 42. Once you have this right, you can finish it. Push up with your hands in a circular motion and bend your body to the left for added power. This will release the stranglehold. Once you have released the hold, you must remember that the attacker has not been stunned! He is still able to continue the attack! So get away *fast*. You could start this escape method with a front kick to the groin if you wished; it's up to you. The front kick would stun him and make it easier to escape.

I have described three different methods to escape from the straight arm strangle. Try them all. Choose the two that work best for you. Only *you* can decide what suits *you* best. Accept your own judgement. As long as the methods you chose work for *you* that is all that is important.

As you are practising these escape methods, you may well find that you can vary them slightly to make them even more effective. If this is the case then that's fine, do it. You may even find that you can invent your own methods and that's fine too. But just a word of caution. Try to keep your methods simple and uncomplicated. One or two moves is always better than five or six. The quicker you escape the better.

SUMMARY

This summary assumes that you are going to begin the escape with your left arm.
1. Take your left arm over the top of the attacker's right arm and underneath his left.
2. Make sure that your left elbow is above his right elbow and your left hand is below his left elbow.
3. Bend your knees slightly as you place your left hand in the correct position and grip it with your right.
4. Push upwards in a circular motion with your hands and straighten your legs at the same time. The hold should now be released.
5. *Run!*

BENT ARM STRANGLE

If you go back and look at Figure 33 you can see that this stranglehold is applied slightly differently. The attacker's arms are bent and he is much closer to the victim. Though the victim is still being strangled, the application of the hold is different. How then can you escape from this type of stranglehold? Well, you could try the escape methods I described for the straight arm strangle, and they may work well for you, but I doubt if the 'S' type method will work very well this time. Because the attacker's arms are bent, you may not be able to get your hands underneath his arms. I also doubt if you could kick the attacker's groin because he is much too close to you. The first method of escape from the straight arm strangle (bending his fingers back) will probably work, as will the second method (arm over like a windmill), but I don't like to take chances, so here are a few methods to escape from the bent arm strangle.

Bent Arm Strangle Escape No. 1

Because the attacker is much closer to you in this type of attack, more possibilities of escape are opened up. Look at Figure 33. The very first thing that comes to mind in order to escape from this type of attack doesn't need much explanation or practice. The victim could very easily grip the attacker's hips with both hands and raise one of her knees into his groin. The force of the blow would be enough to make him release his grip.

HOW TO PRACTISE

Get your partner to apply the hold as shown in Figure 33. Now place both of your hands onto his hips and grip them tightly. Then *very slowly* and *gently,* raise one of your knees up toward his groin. *Do not* make contact. Just get the feel of the movement *without* making contact.

In a real attack you would raise your knee as fast and as hard as you could, thrusting into the attacker's groin. Very few men can withstand a blow of that force. Ask your husband or boyfriend what effect a blow of that kind would do to them. They'll probably cringe and cross their knees at the very thought of it. When a man suffers a blow to his groin, he will normally lean forward from the hips, knees together, clutching his masculinity with his hands. He will be unable to breathe or walk properly. This will give you the time you need to escape and get help, if not for yourself, then for the attacker.

SUMMARY
1. Grip the attacker's hips with both of your hands.
2. Pull the attacker's hips into your body and raise your knee into his groin.
3. *Run!*

Bent Arm Strangle Escape No. 2

Another simple method you can employ from the bent arm strangle is to stun the attacker with the heels of your hands. Figure 33 shows the bent arm strangle. You can see that the victim would have no problem using her hands to strike to the attacker's head. The only problem is deciding how to strike. A simple slap across the face might well sound effective but, in reality, it is very doubtful whether this would make the attacker release his grip. Instead of a slap across the face, why not use two strikes at the same time? And instead of slapping with the palms of your hands, strike with the heels of your hands. All you have to do is swing both of your hands at the same time. If you can strike the attacker's ears, it will do one of three things:

      1. Stun him.
      2. Knock him unconscious.
      3. Kill him.

Let us move on to the best way to practise this method.

HOW TO PRACTISE
Get your partner to apply the hold as shown in Figure 33. All you have to do now is to make sure you can strike to both of the attacker's ears at the same time.

The first thing to do is to arch your hands backwards. Keep both of your hands by your side when you arch them. Now, *very slowly* and *very gently* swing both of your hands up to the attacker's ears. *Do not make contact*

when you practise. Just make sure that you *can* strike the targets at the same time. Obviously, in a real situation you would strike the targets as quickly as possible.

This striking method is very simple and *very effective.* If you are forced to use it, then you should push the attacker away from you as soon as you have stunned him.

SUMMARY
1. Keeping both of your arms by your sides, arch both of your hands backwards. Keep both of your arms straight as you arch your hands.
2. Keeping both arms straight, swing them both up to the attacker's head and strike his ears with the heels of both hands.
3. *Run!*

Bent Arm Strangle Escape No. 3

The last method I am going to describe is a double movement method. When used correctly it is very possible to dislocate the attacker's shoulder and, should you feel the need, leave the attacker in a very dangerous position. Figure 33 shows the attack.

Now look at Figure 44. The victim has moved her left arm under both of the attacker's arms and gripped his left elbow with her left hand. She has also placed her right hand onto the right side of his head/face. From this position, all she has to do now is to pull her left hand across her body, and pull her right hand in the opposite direction.

Figure 45 shows the outcome of these two pulling movements and also the victim's knee poised to strike the attacker's head. Should the victim use a maximum power strike to the attacker's head, she would cause severe injury and possibly even kill him.

HOW TO PRACTISE
Get your partner to apply the bent arm strangle as shown in Figure 33. Move your left arm underneath both of the attacker's arms and grip his/her left elbow from the underside. Move your right hand on to the

44

45

right side of the attacker's head/face. Your hands should both move into position at the same time. Practise that part of the escape first. Start slowly at first, building up your speed gradually. When you find that you can move both of your hands into position very quickly, you can add the final part of the escape. Check with Figure 44 to make absolutely certain that you are in the correct position before completing the escape.

With your hands positioned correctly, you are now going to pull the attacker's arm and head in alternate directions. Your left hand pulls the attacker's left elbow across your body from *your* right to left. You right hand pulls the attacker's head across your body from *your* left to right.

Both of these pulling movements are done at the same time. When you are practising, do them *very, very slowly.* If you pull too quickly in practise you may dislocate your partner's shoulder.

Figure 45 shows the completed escape. In the photograph, the victim's knee has been raised to strike the attacker's head. In practise sessions, *take it easy* when you raise your knee. If you feel that you are likely to strike with your knee during practise then *don't raise your knee.* A knee strike to the head will cause serious injury or death. You must exercise complete control when you practise. *Be careful.*

SUMMARY
This summary assumes that you are going to start the escape with your left hand.
1. Your left arm moves underneath the attacker's arms and your hand grips his left elbow from the underneath.
2. Your right hand moves above the attacker's arms to the right side of his head/face.
3. Two movements done at the same time: your left hand pulls the attacker's left elbow across your body from right to left; your right hand pulls the attacker's head/face across your body from left to right.
4. As you pull the attacker's head across your body, you may wish to use a knee strike to his head. Raise your knee to the attacker's head as you pull it across your body.
5. *Run!*

CONCLUSION

I have described six different methods to escape from strangleholds. Some of them may seem very harsh in that they will cause an attacker considerable distress. The reason for this is very simple; if a man is trying to strangle you, it is because he wants to *kill* you. You must be harsh because you won't get a second chance. You are dealing with a lunatic who will *kill* you if you don't escape. You have to be quick and very effective. If being effective means that you have to injure him, then surely that is better than being dead?

The escape methods I have described will work for other types of attack as well. For instance, if a man was holding you by gripping your clothing close to your neck, the same escape methods would probably work equally well. Try it out for yourself. Get your partner to hold your clothing close to your neck or chest and try the escape methods you have just practised. Remember to use care when escaping. Don't hurt your partner.

The double strike with the heels of your hands (to the attacker's ears) can be used in many types of attack, so make a mental note of it. You can use it to stun an attacker at any time, as you can with a knee strike to the groin, but obviously you must be close enough to hit the target before you use them.

7 Free Standing Holds~Hugs

The bear hug type of attack is very common. It can be used by the office wolf or the drunken party-goer who thinks that one dance with you is enough to attempt a kiss and cuddle. It is also used in the more serious rape or mugging attacks. Let us take a look at the bear-hug type of attack.

FRONT BEAR HUGS

In the less serious type of attack, the bear hug will normally be applied while you are facing the attacker (Figure 46), usually as though in fun. If this is the case, then it's pretty obvious that you don't want to make the situation worse by injuring the attacker. So, for this type of attack, I will describe a simple escape method which will lighten rather than aggravate the situation.

Front Bear Hug Escape No. 1

Look at Figure 46. The attacker has put his arms around the victim's arms and trapped them just above her elbows. Though her upper arms are trapped, she can still move her lower arms below her elbows. To free herself from the attacker without injuring him, all the victim has to do is tickle the attacker's ribs as though in fun. By tickling the attacker, the victim lightens the situation rather than making it worse.

HOW TO PRACTISE

This escape method doesn't need much practice. Just get your partner to apply the bear hug as shown in Figure 46. The hug should be applied as though in fun. Then simply tickle your way out of it. Try your best to tickle the attacker's ribs, because even those people who are not normally ticklish find it uncomfortable.

SUMMARY

1. Raise both of your hands up to the attacker's ribs and tickle your way free.

46

Front Bear Hug Escape No. 2

The bear hug as shown in Figure 46 can be applied in a more serious type of attack. The next method I am going to describe will get you free very quickly when applied correctly, but it will not injure the attacker.

This time, instead of tickling your way out of the hug, pinch your way out. Once again, this escape method does not require much practice. Its effectiveness lies in its simplicity and the shock it gives to the attacker.

You already know that you can move your arms below the elbow, so all you have to do is move your hands to whichever part of the attacker you want to pinch. Most women find that the attacker's kidney area is an easy target.

HOW TO PRACTISE

Get your partner to apply the bear hug as shown in Figure 46. Make certain that the hug is applied tightly, just as it would be in a serious attack. Now move both of your hands towards the attacker's kidney area. (The attacker will not be able to see what your hands are doing because they are behind his back.) Now, using your fingers and thumbs, pinch the fleshy area around his kidneys. As you pinch into his flesh, you should also twist your hands. By twisting as you pinch, you will add a lot more pain to the attacker's body. As soon as the hold is released *run*.

It must be pointed out that the attacker will not be injured if you use this method of escape. He can still run after you. If he does, then you know how to escape from being chased. We covered that in Chapter 4.

SUMMARY

1. Raise both of your hands up to the attacker's kidney area.

2. Using your index finger and thumb, pinch the fleshy area around his kidneys.

3. As you are pinching the fleshy area around his kidneys, you should also twist your hands to add to his discomfort.

4. As soon as he releases the hold, *run*.

Front Bear Hug Escape No. 3

For those of you who feel that you should stun an attacker in order to escape from the bear hug, then this is also very simple.

Look at Figure 46. You can see that the victim is very close to the attacker. Her upper arms may well be trapped, but her lower arms and her knees and feet are completely free. She could very easily use a knee strike to the attacker's groin, then follow it with a hard stamp onto his feet. Two strikes for the price of one!

HOW TO PRACTISE

You *must* exercise great caution when you practise this escape method. If you strike your partner's groin, it can cause serious injury. Take it easy.

Get your partner to apply the hug as shown in Figure 46. Now, very slowly and very gently place your hands onto his hips and raise one of your knees towards his groin. *Do not* make contact with your knee. Just get the feel of the movement. When you have raised your knee to your partner's groin, then lower your leg gently and stand on one of his feet. Practise that combination of movements until you are getting it right every time, but do it slowly and gently. It is as simple as that, just raise your knee and put it down.

In a real attack, it is up to you how hard you strike. This method will shock, stun and seriously injure the attacker. It is your choice.

SUMMARY

1. Place both of your hands onto the attacker's hips.

2. Raise one of your knees into the attacker's groin.

3. With the raised leg, stamp down onto the attacker's toes.

4. *Run*.

Front Bear Hug Escape No. 4

The last method I shall describe for escaping from a bear hug applied from the front uses a simple throw. If applied correctly, it will put the attacker onto the floor.

Look at Figure 47. The victim has moved her right leg diagonally across her body and placed it behind the attacker's right leg.

Figure 48 shows the same movement from the opposite side. In Figure 48, you can see that the victim's right hand has moved up to the attacker's left armpit. In Figures 47 and 48, you can see that the victim's hips have moved in tight to the attacker's hips.

Now look at Figure 49. The victim has twisted her body in an anti-clockwise direction. As she did so, she bent her left leg and straightened her right leg. The attacker was thrown over the victim's right leg. Once the attacker has been thrown to the floor, the victim would run.

47

48

49

HOW TO PRACTISE

Get your partner to apply the hug as shown in Figure 46. Now look at Figures 47 and 48. Move your right leg behind your partner's right leg or, if you can, place your right leg behind both of the attacker's legs. You should find that a twist of your hips makes it easier to move your right leg into position. As you are moving your right leg into position, move both of your hands up to the attacker's armpits. Practise that part of the escape a few times until it starts to come easy. When you have that part right, you can complete the escape.

Your right leg should be behind the attacker's right leg. Your right hand should be up to the attacker's left armpit. Your left hand should be up to the attacker's right armpit, as shown in Figures 47 and 48.

The last part of the escape will put the attacker onto the floor. With your right hand, which is up to his left armpit, pinch his skin as you did in the previous escape. You will find that his body tries to move away from the pain, i.e. to his right (your left). As his body moves to your left, push him in the same direction with your right hand to help him on his way. As you pinch and push with your right hand, twist your body in an anti-clockwise direction. As you twist your body, bend your left leg and straighten your right. The attacker will be thrown over your right leg. In fact, the attacker is throwing himself. He is throwing himself because he moves away from the pain you inflict when you pinch him.

Look at Figure 49. The completed escape leaves the attacker on the floor. If you want to add a further strike to the attacker while he is in this prone position, then it is up to you. The important thing is that you do escape. Once the attacker is on the floor, this will give you those extra few seconds. Don't be brave, get help!

Now that you know several methods of escape from this type of bear hug you should find that you can mix them around to suit yourself. You may find that you want to use a knee strike and then add the throw. It is up to you. All that is important is that you do escape. Once you are free of the attacker you can get help. Don't be brave, be safe.

SUMMARY

This summary assumes that you use your right leg to begin the escape.

1. Move your right leg diagonally across your body and place your right foot behind the attacker's right foot.

2. Move both of your hands up to the attacker's armpits.

3. Pinch the attacker's skin with your right hand.

4. Push the attacker's body with your right hand from your right to left.

5. As you pinch and push with your right hand, twist your body in an anti-clockwise direction.

6. As you twist your body, bend your left leg and straighten your right.

7. The attacker will be thrown over your straight right leg.

8. When the attacker hits the floor, *run.*

REAR BEAR HUGS

Now that you know several methods of escaping from the bear hug applied from the front, we can go on to escaping from bear hugs applied from the back (Figure 50). This type of attack can be applied in a mild or serious form. I shall describe various methods of escape to deal with both applications.

Rear Bear Hug Escape No. 1

Look at Figure 50. The attacker has applied a bear hug from the back. As with the bear hug from the front, you can see that the victim's upper arms are trapped but her lower arms are free. The victim could escape from this attack by simply pinching her way out. All she has to do is move her hips to the left or right, then pinch whichever part of the attacker's anatomy that comes to hand. In a mild form of attack, you could pinch his thigh or his tummy. In a more serious type of attack, you could, instead of pinching, use a striking method to his groin. A strike to an attacker's groin is normally enough to make him release the hold. I have explained in previous chapters how devastating a strike to the groin can be for a man, but, before you can strike or pinch

50

your way free, you have to know how to get your hands behind your back quickly. So let's move on to the practise section straight away.

HOW TO PRACTISE

The most important part of this escape method is to get your hands working as soon as possible. Whether it is a mild attack, and you are going to pinch your way out, or a serious attack, and you are going to strike your way out, you have got to know how to use your hands quickly and effectively. This is how it is done.

Get your partner to apply a bear hug as shown in Figure 50. Now, let us assume that you want to use your right hand to pinch or strike your way free. Simply rotate your hips clockwise and move them to the left. Look down and you can see that the attacker's groin is wide open to your right hand, as is his right thigh and lower tummy. It's as simple as that. Now all you have to do is pinch or strike your way free. If you want to strike to the attacker's groin then there are two methods which most women find very effective:

1. The hammerfist.
2. The chop/knifehand.

The application of the hammerfist is very simple. All you have to do is clench your fist and assume that your fist is the head of the hammer and your forearm is the handle. You would strike the target with the little finger edge of your fist.

The chop/knifehand is also very simple. All you have to do is keep your fingers straight and keep them together. Tense the whole of your hand and strike the target with the little finger edge of your hand.

When practising, *do not* make contact with the target. Just go through the movements slowly and gently. Choose whichever striking method suits you best. If you want to pinch your way free, then you would simply pinch rather than strike.

If you want to use your left hand to strike or pinch your way free, then you would reverse the first part of the escape. You would twist your hips anti-clockwise and move them to the right.

This twisting escape method offers you three different methods of escape from the bear hug applied from the rear. In a real attack situation, it would be up to you to decide which one to use. Remember that, if you just pinch your way free, then the attacker would still be able to continue the attack. So use the pinching method only in the milder type of attack. The striking methods will cause severe pain and shock the attacker. If the attacker doesn't release you after the first strike, keep on striking until he does. One accurate strike is far better than a thousand near misses!

SUMMARY

This summary assumes that you are going to use your right hand to effect the escape.

1. Rotate your hips clockwise and move them to the left.
2. Look down and choose which target to strike or pinch.
3. Strike or pinch your chosen target as hard as you can.
4. *Run.*

Rear Bear Hug Escape No. 2

Another simple method which you can use to escape from this attack is to bend the attacker's little finger backwards or his thumb into itself. To bend his little finger backwards, simply move your hands up to the attacker's hands and pick the nearest little finger you can see, then bend it backwards away from your body. The attacker will have to move his hand in the same direction as you are bending his little finger in order to ease the pain. To do so, he obviously has to release the hug. Once you have released the hug, it's up to you whether you add a further strike to the attacker or simply talk your way out of the situation.

To escape from this attack by bending the attacker's thumb into itself, move your hands up to the attacker's hands as in the previous escape and choose whichever thumb is on top. Look at Figure 51. The attacker's right hand is on top. The victim is pushing the tip of the attacker's right thumb with her left thumb, forcing it into itself. She has clamped his right hand with her right hand for stability. She pushes the tip of his thumb as hard as she can, so that his thumb bends into itself. When applied correctly this causes very severe pain to

the attacker and, in order to escape the pain, he has to release the hug.

HOW TO PRACTISE

Get your partner to apply the bear hug as shown in Figure 50. Now look for either a little finger or a thumb. If you can see a little finger, simply bend it backwards away from your body. As the attacker's hand moves away from your body, step forward. Keep bending his little finger as you step forward and there you are, free. Should you wish to apply a further strike to the attacker, you will probably find that a back kick flows very easily.

If you can see a thumb when the hold is applied all you have to do is bend the thumb into itself. Have Figure 51 in front of you when you practise the thumb method of escape. Assuming that your attacker has his right hand on top, clamp his right hand with your right hand. Then with your left thumb, push the tip of his right thumb into the underside of its own knuckle. This will cause severe pain to the attacker's thumb; the only way he can ease the pain is to release the hold. As soon as the hold has been released, it's up to you to decide if any further action is required. You may find that a back kick flows very easily with this escape method.

Bending an attacker's thumb into itself causes severe pain but seldom causes injury. It's more of a shock than anything else and it can be used to escape from many other types of attack as well as the rear bear hug. Practise this method until you get it right every time. Then practise it with your eyes closed so that you can feel your way out of it. You will be surprised how effective it is and how quickly your attacker releases you.

SUMMARY

Little finger escape:

1. Grip the attacker's little finger with one of your hands and bend it backwards away from your body.

2. As the attacker's hand moves away from your body, step forward.

3. (Optional) Use a back kick to the attacker's body once you have stepped forward.

4. *Run.*

Thumb escape:

This summary assumes that the attacker's right hand is above his left.

1. Clamp the attacker's right hand with your right hand.

2. Using your left thumb, push the tip of his right thumb into itself so that you are forcing the fingerprint side of his thumb into the underside of its own knuckle.

3. (Optional) When the hold has been released use a back kick to the attacker's body.

4. *Run.*

Rear Bear Hug Escape No. 3

Look at Figure 50. You can see that the victim's legs and feet are completely free. If the victim wanted to, she could easily shock and stun the attacker with her feet. It is very easy to strike the attacker's groin when held in a bear hug from the back. It is just as easy to strike to his feet. If you wanted to, you could use both strikes as one combined movement, striking firstly to his groin then onto his feet. Let us move straight into the practise section and find out how to do it with maximum effect.

HOW TO PRACTISE

I don't recommend practising these two striking methods with a partner, because the slightest error in judgement could cause severe injury.

These two shock/stun methods don't require much practise, but will cause extreme pain to the attacker when used correctly. To strike the attacker's groin, you should start by trying to kick you own backside with the back of your heel. Do *not* raise your knee in front of you as you do with a front kick. Keep your knee down. Just flick your heel up to your bottom. Once you find that you can kick your own backside, you shouldn't have much trouble kicking to an attacker's groin.

To practise striking down onto the attacker's feet, start by raising your knee in front of you, as you do in the front kick, then kick down with the base of your heel onto the attacker's feet.

To practise the two strikes as a combination is simplicity itself. Start with the groin strike first. Raise the back of your heel into your own backside, then without putting your foot back onto the floor, raise your knee to the front and strike down. It's as easy as that. Groin strike first, raise your knee to the front, foot strike second – two strikes almost at the same time. So there you are, two more striking methods to add to your ever-increasing list of alternatives.

SUMMARY

1. Raise one of your heels behind you and strike the attacker's groin.

2. When you have struck the attacker's groin, raise the knee of your striking leg in front of you.

3. Strike down onto the attacker's feet with your raised leg. Use your heel to strike.

4. *Run.*

Rear Bear Hug Escape No. 4

Now that you know several methods of striking an attacker to escape from the rear hug, I will describe two methods which, if used correctly, will leave the attacker shocked, stunned, in pain and on the floor. These two methods should only be used in the more serious types of attack and, when practising, great care should be taken not to injure your partner. Figure 50 shows the beginning of the rear hug attack.

Look at Figure 52. The victim has moved her right leg diagonally behind her left leg and she has placed her right foot on the floor beside the attacker's left leg. As she moved her right leg into position, she also used a hand strike to the attacker's groin to shock him.

Now look at Figure 53. The victim's right leg is straight and she is spinning on her feet in a clockwise motion. Her feet stay in the same position on the floor as she spins. Her right arm is pushing against the attacker's body as she spins. Her right leg acts as a trip wire on the attacker's left leg.

In Figure 54, you can see that the attacker is tripping over the victim's right leg and he has released his grip. His hands are reaching out behind him – a completely involuntary action on his part, but a natural one. In falling, his natural reaction is to protect himself from the fall. As soon as the attacker has gone down, the victim

52

53

54

doesn't wait to see the outcome, she runs as fast as she can away from the attacker to get help!

HOW TO PRACTISE

The first step in this escape method is the diagonal leg movement. Look at Figure 52. Get your partner to hold you lightly in a rear hug, now take your right leg behind your left and put it down beside your attacker's left leg. Practise this move until you can do it easily. Once it starts getting easy, get your attacker to hold you tighter and tighter until he is holding you as tight as he/she can. Once you can get your right leg into position with your attacker holding you as tightly as possible, you can add some more. Now, as you move your right leg into position, go through the motions of a hand strike to the groin while you move your leg, i.e. as your right leg moves into position you strike your attacker's groin with your right hand, combining two moves – hand and leg. When you have managed to get that right you are halfway there. Be very careful not to strike your attacker in the groin when you are practising.

Now look at Figure 53. With your right leg in the correct position, spin in a clockwise motion and straighten your right leg as you spin. Your feet remain in the same position on the floor as you spin. You should be pushing the attacker's body with your right hand and arm as you spin clockwise. Figure 54 shows the completed escape with the attacker going over your right leg. It is very important that you start slowly and gently when practising this escape method. If you rush it you may well hurt your partner.

Once you are getting it right every time, try and do it with your eyes closed. If you practise it this way, you will teach yourself to feel your way out, rather than fight your way out.

It is a good idea to practise with more than one partner as this will help you to understand the importance of technique, rather than strength, in escaping from an attacker who is much bigger and stronger than you.

SUMMARY

N.B. This summary assumes that you begin this escape with your right leg.

1. Move your right leg diagonally behind your left and place your right foot beside your attacker's left foot (on the outside of his left foot).

2. (Optional) You may strike to the attacker's groin as you are moving your right leg.

3. Spin your body in a clockwise direction and straighten your right leg as you spin.

4. As you spin your body, use your right arm and hand to push the attacker over your right leg.

5. As soon as the attacker is on the floor, *run.*

Rear Bear Hug Escape No. 5

This last method will, if applied correctly, leave the attacker on the floor completely at your mercy.

Figure 50 shows the attack. The victim would immediately use either a shock or stun method to begin the escape. We will assume that the victim has raised her right leg behind her and used her heel to strike the attacker's groin. Then, as she brings her foot down, she also stamps down hard onto the attacker's toes.

Now look at Figure 55. After striking the attacker's right toes, the victim places her right foot to the side of the attacker's right foot and leans her body forward. As she leans forward, she reaches behind her (between her legs) and grabs the attacker's right ankle. She is able to lean forward and reach behind her, because the two strikes to the attacker's groin and toes, have made the attacker loosen his grip.

Now look at Figure 56. The victim has lifted the attacker's right foot between her legs and is resting her elbows on her knees. Note the way the victim is holding the attacker's foot: both of her hands are underneath his ankle, her knees are slightly bent, her elbows are resting on her knees.

Now look at Figure 57. The victim has done several things. She has simply sat on her attacker's thigh as though squatting and, at the same time, pulled upwards on his ankle with her hands: the effect of these combined movements can be seen. The attacker is on the floor, his legs are wide apart offering a very delicate target. If the victim wanted to, she could raise her left leg and strike down to the attacker's groin, but that's up to her isn't it?

55

HOW TO PRACTISE

The first step in this escape method is to shock and stun the attacker. Start by raising your right foot into his groin and then stamping down onto his toes. Obviously, you can't strike a partner in this way, but you can still go through the motions without actually making contact. Assuming you have done this, the next step is to place your right foot down beside the attacker's right foot and, at the same time, lean forward, reaching behind you for the attacker's right ankle, Figure 55 shows the correct position. Practise that part of the escape until you are getting it right and make sure you go through the motions of striking first. When you find that you can easily grab your attacker's ankle, try getting your elbows onto your knees, as in Figure 55. Practise those two movements until they are coming easily. When you are this far you can complete the escape.

Look at Figure 57. The completion of this escape is similar to a see-saw effect: your hands pulling up are one end of the see-saw, your elbows resting on your knees

56

57

are the centre point of the see-saw and your bottom, sitting on the attacker's thigh, is the other end of the see-saw. Your hands pull up, your bottom pushes down. When you start to practise this part of the escape, you will find that you can feel the attacker start to go down. At this point, you must immediately stand up, pulling on the attacker's ankle as hard as you can. This will ensure that he goes down quickly with his legs apart. Once the attacker is on the floor, the rest is up to you. You've already shocked and stunned him, so you should have time to escape and get help.

SUMMARY

N.B. This summary assumes that you use your right leg to begin the escape.

1. Raise your right heel into the attacker's groin and then stamp down onto his toes.

2. After stamping on his toes, place your right foot down beside your attacker's right foot (your right foot to the outside of your attacker's right foot).

3. Lean forward from the waist, reach behind you and grip the attacker's right ankle.

4. Rest your elbows on your kness and pull on the attacker's ankle.

5. As you pull up on the attacker's ankle, push down on his leg with your bottom.

6. As the attacker goes down behind you, straighten your legs and stand up straight still holding on to the attacker's ankle with both of your hands.

7. (Optional) As the attacker will be on the floor behind you with his legs apart, you may use a back kick to the attacker's groin if you think it is necessary.

8. *Run.*

CONCLUSION

Many of the escape methods from the bear hug type of attack have required a strike to the attacker's body. It is unfortunate, but also very necessary. In order to escape from an attacker, who will usually be much bigger and stronger than you are, you have to loosen his grip in some way before you can complete the escape. It is therefore very important that you get used to either shocking or stunning an attacker so that you can implement the escape methods described in this section of the book.

You may find that you can mix the various escape methods described and come up with another, different, type of escape from the bear hug attacks. If you can, that's fine. It proves that you are thinking for yourself and that's the way it's going to be in a real attack – just you, thinking for yourself. The only advice I offer if you are inventing your own methods of escape is to keep them as simple and as quick as possible and, of course, make sure they are effective.

8 Free Standing Holds ~Arm Holds

It is not unusual for an attacker to hold his victim by the arms in some way and this chapter deals with the various methods you can employ to escape from this type of hold. In a serious attack situation, the victim will usually try to strike the attacker, normally by hammering on the attacker's chest with her fists. In order to stop this, the attacker will grip his victim's arms tightly. He may use a bear-hug type of hold (which we dealt with in Chapter 7) or try to use his strength to hold the victim's arms still.

It is also very common for an attacker to hold only one of his victim's arms with one hand, while his other hand is trying to remove the victim's, or his own, clothing. Similarly, the attacker may well use both hands or arms to hold only one of the victim's arms. No matter how the attacker chooses to hold the victim's arms, one thing is certain; he is holding them to stop the victim from hurting him. So, armed with this knowledge (i.e. that the attacker is scared), I will describe some methods to escape from a stronger, bigger, attacker who holds both your arms.

If you look at Figures 58-60, you can see the three most common arm holds. Figure 58 shows the attacker holding the victim's arms down. Figure 59 shows the attacker holding the victim's arms up. Figure 60 shows the attacker using both of his arms to hold only one of the victim's arms.

ARMS DOWN HOLDS

I will deal firstly with Figure 58. The attacker is holding the victim's arms down. Look closely at this Figure and you can see that the attacker's thumbs are above the victim's thumbs. It is very important that you make a mental note of this positioning of the thumbs, because I am going to describe a way of escape by going through the attacker's thumbs. Still looking at Figure 58, can you see any way in which you could shock or stun the attacker to loosen his grip?

Hopefully, you will have thought of perhaps a knee strike to the attacker's groin or even a kick. Maybe a good hard stamp onto his toes or even his knees or shins. All are good shock and stun methods, but there is another way you could try without using your hands or legs. It is a method which you may find filthy and disgusting, but if you are already thinking of using a knee or kick to the groin, then it's not really that bad. After all, this guy is going to rape and possibly kill you. It is a method I first discovered in Aldershot. A young WRAC recruit was being harrassed by a young intoxicated soldier. He had grabbed her by the arms, just as in Figure 58, and her immediate reaction was to *spit in his face*. The young soldier was caught offguard for just long enough for the WRAC recruit to make her escape; she didn't need to do anything else except run. It may not be very pleasant but it is very, very effective. So here is another to add to your already growing list of shock and stun techniques.

58

59

60

Arms Down Hold Escape No. 1

In order to escape from this type of hold, the victim firstly shocks or stuns the attacker in some way; choose your own method. Look at Figure 61. The victim has twisted both of her arms inwards, her right arm twisting in a clockwise direction and her left arm twisting anti-clockwise. Her upper arms (biceps) do not move as she twists out of the hold. Her arms twist out from the elbow down, out through the attacker's thumbs. Once the victim has escaped from the hold, she *runs.*

HOW TO PRACTISE

First of all, your partner should hold your arms lightly, so that you get the feel of the twisting movement. Your partner should hold your arms down, as in Figure 58. Now, assuming that you have shocked or stunned the attacker in some way, the rest is easy. Keep your upper arms (biceps) rigid and twist both of your arms inwards, your left arm rotating anti-clockwise, your right arm

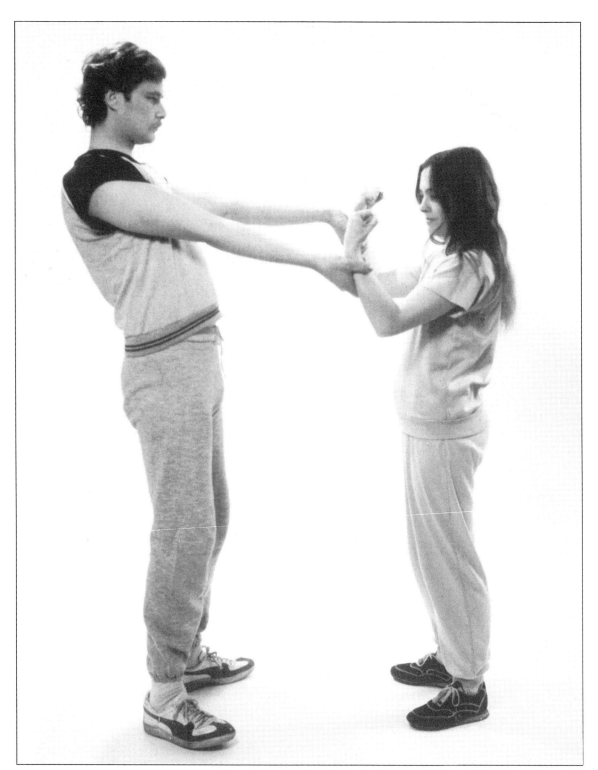

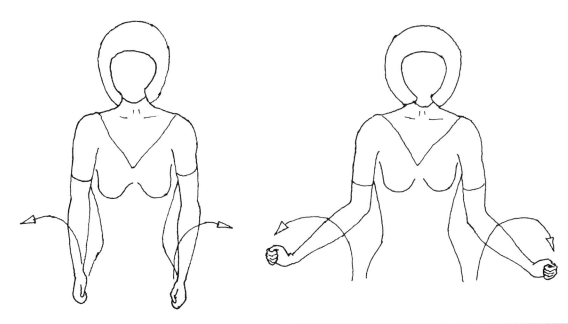

rotating clockwise. Both of your arms move at the same time: inwards until they are level with each other and then outwards in a circular motion. Look at the diagram (above) so that you move your arms correctly.

Each time you practise this escape method, you must go through the motions of shocking or stunning the attacker before you twist out of the hold. As always, you should take care not to make contact when you are practising with a partner.

SUMMARY

1. Shock or stun the attacker.
2. Twist both of your arms inwards in a circular motion. Your left arm moves anti-clockwise and your right arm clockwise.
3. *Run.*

Arms Down Hold Escape No. 2

Another escape from the same hold which you may like to try is designed for the very serious attack situation. This method will stun your attacker at the very least, although it is more likely to knock him unconscious. It should only be used as a very last resort.

Taking the same attack situation shown in Figure 58,

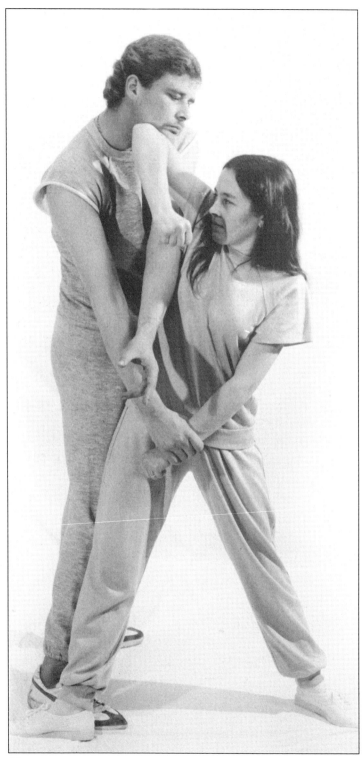

63

this alternative method involves stepping diagonally across your body.

Look at Figure 62. The victim has moved her right leg diagonally across her body and put it down beside the attacker's right leg. As she moved her right leg across her body, she also threw her right arm across the top of her left arm, as though she was punching across her body. The victim's right arm is now free from the attacker's grip, her right hip is tight into the attacker's thighs, her right arm is straight. The next movement is the one that does the damage.

Look at Figure 63. The victim has pulled her right arm backwards and used an elbow strike into the attacker's head/face. As with any strike, the victim aims the blow to go through and beyond the target for maximum efficiency. As soon as the victim has escaped from the attacker, she runs to get help. She doesn't wait around to see the outcome.

HOW TO PRACTISE

In order to succeed in this escape method, it is very important that your right hand and leg move at the same time. First of all, practise the escape without a partner. Start by standing with your feet as wide apart as your shoulders. Then move your right leg across the front of your left leg and, at the same time, throw a punch with your right arm, also across your body, to the left. The leg movement diagram (below) will help you move into the correct position. Punch and step at the same time. When you have practised this a few times, get your

partner to hold your arms as in Figure 58. Then go through the same movement again, making sure that your right arm moves across the top of your left arm. You must step and punch at the same time. When you can escape easily from your partner, then go on to practising the elbow strike, but *don't* make contact; just go through the motions of striking the target. You must take great care when practising this strike, because it is very dangerous.

You will probably find that the attacker only releases your right arm as you step across your body. If that happens, don't worry; it is to your benefit because, if the attacker is still holding your left arm as you have stepped across, you can use it to pull your striking arm into the target. Figure 63 shows more clearly what I mean. You can see that the attacker is still holding the victim's left arm, even though she has stepped across her body and released her right arm. All she does now is to use his grip on her left arm to stabilise her body as she winds back into the elbow strike. The attacker uses his own grip to aid the victim's escape.

SUMMARY

N.B. This summary assumes that you begin the escape with your right leg.

1. Your right arm and leg move at the same time. Move your right leg across the front of your left leg. Throw a punch across the top of your left arm.

2. Strike backwards with your right elbow into the attacker's head/face.

3. *Run.*

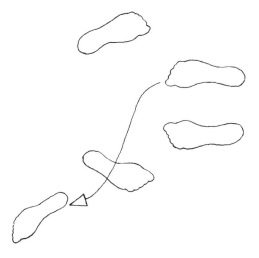

ARMS UP HOLDS

Looking at Figure 59 you can see that the attacker is holding the victim's arms upwards. We can now go on to escaping from this type of hold using an escape similar to that used before. The last escape method we used (the step across method) will probably work very well to escape from the hold in Figure 59. The arm twisting method will *not* work for this hold. It won't work because the victim's arms are already in the final position of that escape, but she can use a similar type of escape, by reversing the twisting. Instead of twisting her arms upwards through the attacker's thumbs, she can escape by twisting her arms downwards and then upwards. She can twist her arms down and then up, so that her arms are on the outside of the attacker's arms. So, you can escape from this type of hold by using escape methods almost identical to those used previously.

64

Arms Up Hold Escape No. 1

There is another way to escape from this type of hold. Do you remember the hugs section where we used a simple throwing technique to floor the attacker. Well I will now describe the same throw from this type of hold. Figure 59 shows the hold we are going to escape from.

Now look at Figure 64. The victim has stepped diagonally across her body with her right leg, putting it down behind the attacker's right leg. If you look at Figure 65, you will see that the victim has pulled her left arm backwards and moved her right arm above the attackers left arm so that she is using her elbow to push against the attacker's head. As the victim is positioning her arms, she is also twisting her body in an anti-clockwise rotation. Figure 66 shows what happens when the victim keeps twisting in this direction.

HOW TO PRACTISE

Practise the step across method just as you did before, making sure that you shock or stun the attacker to loosen his grip. To practise the arm twisting method, start by shocking or stunning the attacker, again to loosen his grip. Then, twist your arms downwards through a full

65

66

360°. Your arms move down the inside of the attacker's arms and up the outside of his arms. To practise the throwing method, start by shocking or stunning the attacker: knee, kick or spit, whichever you prefer. When practising, be careful not to hurt your partner when you shock/stun. Just go through the motion of it, so that if you do need to escape in a real attack situation, you won't need to think of shocking or stunning, you will do it naturally.

Now, with your partner holding your arms (as in Figure 59), and assuming that you have shocked/stunned the attacker, step diagonally across your body with your right leg, placing it behind the attacker's right leg. Do that until it comes easily. Figure 64 shows the position your leg should be in. Now add the following arm and hand movements to the diagonal step. Pull your left arm backwards as you step and, at the same time, roll your right arm over the attacker's left arm so that your right elbow is into his face or neck. Look at Figure 64. This shows the correct positions of your right leg and your left arm. Figure 65 shows the correct position of your right elbow. Now you can

practise three movements together: step with your right leg, pull backwards with your left arm and roll your right elbow over your partner's left arm and into his head. Practise that combination until you are doing it easily.

Once you have progressed this far you can add the final touches that make it really effective. Up to now, the attacker should still be holding your arms so, in order to release his grip completely, you add the following movements. As you are pulling backwards with your left arm, you should be able to grip his right arm with your left hand. Try it for yourself. Now you can complete the escape. Step diagonally with your right leg, pull backwards with your left arm, gripping his right arm with your left hand as you pull, roll your right elbow over his left arm, placing it into his face or neck. Now for the completion: twist your body in an anti-clockwise direction, still pulling his right arm with your left hand, and push your right elbow hard into his face/neck as you twist. Figure 66 shows the outcome of the whole combination.

It should be pointed out that, very often, a knee or kick to the attacker's groin, is enough to make him release you. You could try a kick to the attacker's groin and then just pull your arms away from him. As soon as the attacker has released you, *run!* When the attacker is on the floor, you will have those extra few seconds you need to get away and get help.

You should also practise escaping from this hold by beginning with a diagonal step with your left leg. In other words, use both sides of your body. All you have to do is reverse the sequence, left for right and right for left etc. It doesn't matter which side of your body you use. Use the side that is most comfortable for you.

SUMMARY
N.B. This summary assumes you are going to use your right leg to begin the escape.
1. Shock or stun the attacker.
2. Three movements: step diagonally across your body with your right leg and place it down behind the attacker's right leg, pull your left arm backwards, roll your right elbow across the attacker's left arm and into his head.

3. Grip the attacker's right arm with your left hand.
4. Three movements: twist your body in an anti-clockwise direction, pull his right arm with your left hand, push your right elbow into his head.
5. *Run.*

TWO ARMS AGAINST ONE HOLD

Having dealt with two of the common types of arm holding, I will deal now with the final hold in this section.

Look at Figure 60. The attacker is holding the victim's left arm with both of his hands. This attacker has got to be crazy! The opportunities open to the victim to stun the attacker are countless. Both of the attacker's arms are busy holding only one of the victim's arms. The victim has one arm free to use as she wishes. She could use the heel of her free hand to strike at the attacker's ear (as you did in the strangles section). In a less serious type of attack, she could use her free hand to pinch the attacker's skin or tickle his ribs; the list of possibilities are endless. Try and think of some for yourself. To begin with, I will describe a method of escape which shouldn't hurt the attacker.

Two Arms Against One Hold Escape No. 1

Look at Figure 67. The victim has reached forward and gripped her left hand with her right. As she gripped her left hand, she bent her knees slightly and clenched her left hand into a fist before she gripped it with her right.

Now look at Figure 68. The victim has done several things. She has pulled her left hand with her right and, at the same time, straightened her legs for added power. As she pulled her left hand with her right, she kept her left arm bent at an angle of about 45° so that she pulled it in a circular motion. As you can see, the attacker's arms are raised slightly above his body, offering many targets to the victim should she decide to use a further strike to stun him.

HOW TO PRACTISE

Get your partner to hold your left arm as in Figure 60. Now reach forward and grip your left fist with your right hand, bending your knees slightly as you reach for your fist.

Look at Figure 67. This shows you the correct position. As you grip your left fist, push it down. In pushing it down, the attacker should retaliate by trying to stop you; he should pull up. When he pulls up, you go with his upward force and also pull up in a circular motion. Make sure that your left arm is bent at an angle of about 45° as you pull out of the hold. This aids leverage. As you are pulling out of the hold, straighten your legs. This adds to your power. Once you have escaped from the hold, *run!*

You should also practise escaping from this hold with your right arm held by the attacker. All you have to do is reverse it, left for right and *vice versa*.

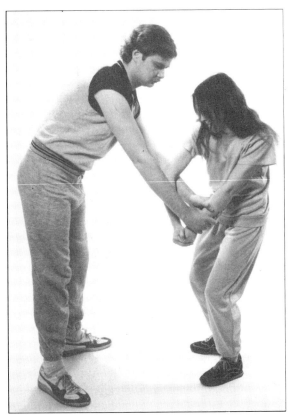

67

SUMMARY

This escape assumes your left arm is being held.

1. Two movements: reach forward and grip your left fist with your right hand; bend your knees slightly as you reach forward.

2. Push your left fist down with your right hand.

3. As the attacker retaliates, pull your left arm upwards in a circular motion and straighten your legs.

4. (Optional) Once the hold has been released you should be able to shock or stun the attacker.

5. *Run.*

Two Arms Against One Hold
Escapes Nos 2 and 3

There are various types of methods you can use to escape from this type of hold and they don't need much practice. For instance, do you remember the strangles section when you bent the attackers fingers backwards? Well you could use the same bending action to release an attacker's grip in this type of attack. All you have to do is pick one of his fingers with your free hand and bend it backwards. Or you could bend the attacker's thumb into itself as you did in the bear hugs section. That should be enough to make the attacker release the hold.

HOW TO PRACTISE

If you choose to bend an attacker's fingers backwards, then it is very important that you hold the finger correctly. The application is slightly different from the stranglehold. Look at Figure 69. This time the victim has her thumb at the tip (on the finger print) of the attacker's finger and her fingers are placed at the attacker's knuckle. Make sure that you keep the attacker's hand close to your body as you bend it backwards. Bend his finger backwards and at the same time, take his hand downwards, just as you did in the strangles section. The outcome will be the same; he will end up on the floor if you apply it correctly.

If you choose to bend the attacker's thumb into itself, then once again the application is slightly different than the previous time you used this method.

Look at Figure 70. This time the victim uses her thumb to bend the attacker's thumb into itself. It is important that you bend the attacker's thumb tip into its own knuckle if this method is to be effective. Applied correctly, this method is very painful but seldom causes injury. The attacker will release the hold in order to ease the pain.

70

SUMMARY

Finger bending backwards:

1. Place the thumb of your free hand at the tip of the attacker's finger (on the fingerprint side) and your fingers at the attacker's knuckle.

2. Keeping the attacker's hand close to your body bend his finger backwards and downwards.

3. *Run.*

Thumb bending:

1. Place the thumb of your free hand onto the tip of the attacker's thumb (on the fingernail side).

2. Push the tip of his thumb into its own knuckle.

3. *Run.*

CONCLUSION

The arm holds which I have described in this chapter deal with the attacker who uses both of his arms to hold his victim. I have not dealt with the attacker who uses only one arm, because that type of attack comes in the following chapter.

You may find that you can mix the escape methods I have described and come up with an escape method of your own design. For instance, you may decide to use the twisting out method, but instead of twisting out with both of your arms, you may prefer to twist out with only one and then follow it with an elbow strike to the attacker's head/face to stun him. Well, if that's your choice, then fine, do it. But a word of caution. If you mix the escape methods, try to keep it simple and effective. If you can free one of your arms from an attacker's grip, then you have far more possibilities of completely escaping the hold.

There are many ways you can escape from an attacker who uses two arms to hold you. You can find many escape methods for yourself. Get your partner to hold you as in Figure 60. Now, can you see any possibilities? Try and think for yourself. If you can't, I'll try and help you. If your partner is holding you very close, do you think you could use a powerful knee strike to his/her groin? Or, could you use an elbow strike to his/her head or neck? If you are being held not too close, could you use a front kick to his/her groin or solar plexus? What about a side kick to his/her knee, or stomach? Perhaps you could stamp down hard onto his/her toes and then follow it with a knee or elbow strike? All of these methods of stunning will, if applied correctly, cause the attacker considerable distress. Each method should be enough to make the attacker release his grip. In fact, each of those methods are more likely to severely injure the attacker. In view of the severity of these stunning methods, it is not advisable to use your partner as a target. Instead use your partner only to see the possibilities open to you.

9 Free Standing Holds - Wrist and Arm Locks

It is very important that you should know how to apply a wrist lock and an arm lock because, once you are familiar with them, they will get you out of almost every type of hold. They will prove successful time and time again. Applied correctly, they will cause great discomfort to the attacker and also have him at your mercy.

Wrist Lock Application

Look at Figure 71. The attacker is holding the victim with his right hand.

Now look at Figure 72. The victim has moved both of her hands to the attacker's hand. Note the position of the victim's thumbs; they are both into the back of the attacker's hand.

Now look at Figure 73. The victim has twisted the attacker's hand in an anti-clockwise rotation and, at the same time, she has bent the attacker's wrist into itself, palm to wrist. She is keeping the attacker's wrist close to her body and, at the same time, she is forcing the wrist down. By keeping the wrist close and pushing it down hard, she can force the attacker onto the floor. The attacker must go onto the floor because this is the only way in which he can ease the pain in his wrist slightly.

HOW TO PRACTISE

Start by getting your partner to hold your clothing close to your neck. The hold should be applied as in Figure 71. Note the position of the attacker's right hand. The back of his hand is perpendicular (at right angles) to the floor. Your partner *must* apply the hold *exactly* as in Figure 71. Later on, once you have practised the escape, it won't matter what position the back of his hand is in.

Now look at Figure 72. Bring your left hand over the top of the attacker's right hand and apply your left

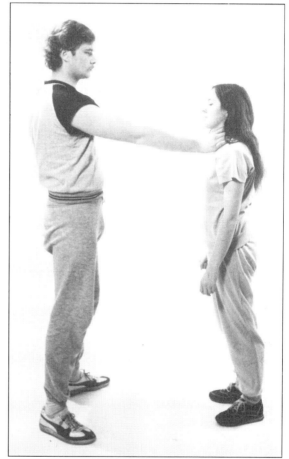

71

thumb to the back of his hand and place the fingers of your left hand into the crease of the attacker's wrist (palm side of *his* hand). At the same time, bring your right hand under the attacker's right hand and place the thumb of your right hand onto the back of the attacker's right hand. The fingers of your right hand also go into the crease of the attacker's right wrist. Study Figure 72 and make certain that you have the position of your

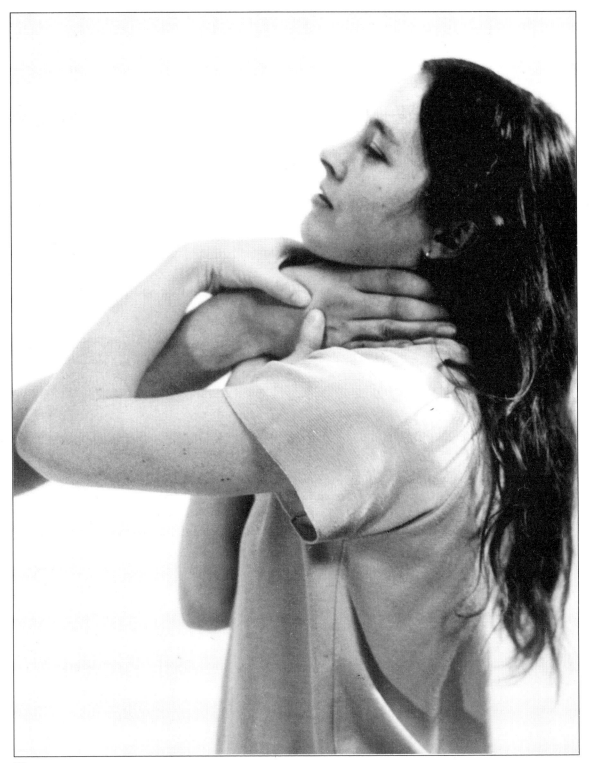

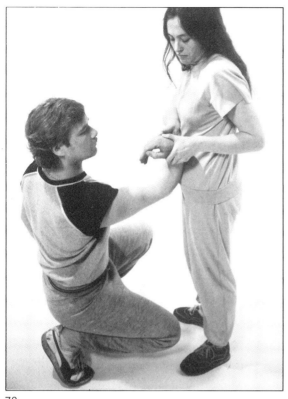

73

hands exactly as the victim in the photograph. Go through the movements slowly at first and gradually build up your speed. *Do not* sacrifice correct application for speed. Your speed will come with practise. Once you are getting the application correct, you can complete the lock.

Now look at Figure 73. This photograph shows the completion of the lock. What you have to do to get this far is to turn your hands slightly in an anti-clockwise motion, roughly about 45°. As you are turning your hands, push hard with your thumbs into the back of the attacker's hand. Make certain that you keep the attacker's hand close to your body as you are pushing hard into the back of his hand with your thumbs. Now, with the lock applied, take the attacker's hand down your body, still pushing hard into his hand with your thumbs. As you take the attacker's hand down your body, try to remain upright; just use your arms to take the attacker down. The lower your hands move, the lower the attacker will go.

Practise this lock until you are getting it right every time. Practise it exactly as I have described, then, get your partner to alter the position of his/her hand, say with the back of his/her hand towards the ceiling, or angled slightly. No matter what the position of the attacker's hand, the application is the same. When you are practising, take it easy. The pain inflicted when you apply a wrist lock is very severe and it is very possible to damage an attacker's wrist when applied correctly.

Get your partner to apply the hold with his/her left hand also. In order to escape and apply the wrist lock, all you need do is reverse it, right for left and *vice versa* etc.

You can also get your partner to apply a similar hold with both hands if you like. The escape is exactly the same. The only difference is that you have a choice of hands to apply the lock to. As you practise escaping from your partner when he/she is using both hands to hold you, get him/her to apply a staggered hold, say, one hand at your neck and the other at your waist, and escape in exactly the same way. *Do* practise this escape until you have it right, because it is going to be used later to escape from other violent forms of attack.

SUMMARY

N.B. This summary assumes that the attacker is holding you with his right hand.

1. Two movements: bring your left hand over the top of the attacker's right hand and apply your left thumb to the back of his hand and place the fingers of your left hand into the crease of the attacker's wrist (palm side of *his* hand); bring your right hand under the attacker's right hand and place the thumb of your right hand onto the back of the attacker's right hand the fingers of your right hand also go into the crease of your attacker's right wrist.

2. Two movements: keeping the attacker's right hand close to your body, twist it in an anti-clockwise direction; push hard with your thumbs into the back of the attacker's hand.

3. Keeping your body upright and the attacker's hand close to your body push it downwards.

4. (Optional) Shock or stun the attacker as he goes down.

5. *Run.*

Arm Lock Application

The arm lock will also get you out of a lot of different situations. As with the wrist lock, it is very important that you can apply it correctly. Let us assume that the attacker is holding the victim in the way shown in Figure 71.

Now look at Figure 74. The victim has moved her right hand over the top of the attacker's right hand and has gripped the attacker's right hand, placing her right thumb into the back of the attacker's right hand. She has placed her fingers into the crease of the attacker's right hand. The victim has used the heel of her left hand to strike hard into the attacker's right elbow and is now holding his elbow with her left hand.

Now look at Figure 75. The victim has twisted her right hand clockwise and applied a wrist lock. At the same time, she pushed hard into the attacker's elbow with her left hand and applied an arm lock. You can see the outcome; the victim has the attacker completely at her mercy.

HOW TO PRACTISE

Start by getting your partner to hold you as in Figure 71. As with the wrist lock, your partner *must* hold you exactly as shown in the photograph to begin with. You can adjust the position of the attacker's hand later on as you progress.

Now look at Figure 74. Move your right hand over the top of the attacker's right hand and place your thumb into the back of his hand. The fingers of your right hand should be in the crease of the attacker's right wrist (palm side of his wrist); you have to roll your right hand completely around the attacker's hand to get it right. Practise this part of the lock a few times until you do get it right. Now, add the strike with the heel of your left hand to the attacker's right elbow. *Do not* make contact when practising with a partner. Just go through the motions of striking the attacker's elbow. The elbow is not a very strong joint and it does not take a lot of power to break it. Be very careful!

Having gone through the motion of striking the attacker's elbow with the heel of your hand, now place

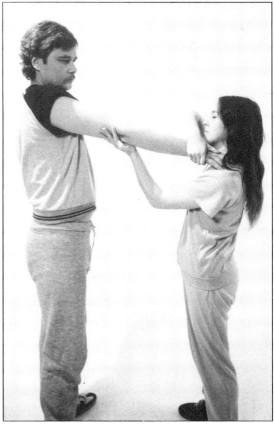

74

your hand onto the attacker's right elbow. You should now be in the same position as the victim in Figure 74. From this position, turn your right hand in a clockwise motion; just do that and nothing else. Practise that a few times until you are getting it right; just turn the attacker's hand clockwise. Get the feel of it. All you are doing is rolling your right hand back into a comfortable position. When you have the feel of the rolling action, you can add a little more.

Now, as you roll your right hand and turn the attacker's right hand, push your thumb into the back of his hand. You should be rolling your hand and pushing into the back of the attacker's hand at the same time. Practise that a few times. Just roll and push with your thumb. You should find that the attacker's hand is bending. What you are actually doing is applying a wrist lock with only one hand. When you have that right, you can add the finishing touches.

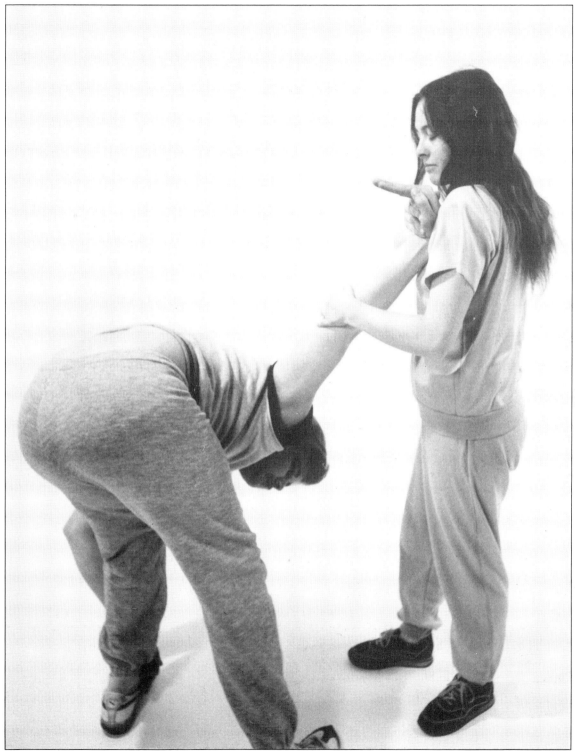

Get your partner to apply the hold as I have described. Now move your hands in the positions shown by the victim in Figure 74. Now, as you roll your right hand and apply the wrist lock, push the attacker's elbow with your left hand. Keep the attacker's right hand close to your body when you roll it back. Your hands move at the same time: your right hand rolling, your left hand pushing; you should push it across and down at an angle of about 45°.

The completed movement is shown in Figure 75. Note the position of the attacker's right hand: his fingers are pointing upward to the ceiling. The victim's thumb is still pushing into the back of his hand. Note the position of the victim's left hand: it is still pushing into the attacker's elbow. So there you are, you have applied a wrist and arm lock at the same time and, what's more, you have the attacker on his knees at your feet. The rest is up to you. You have to decide whether a further strike is necessary or not.

If you want to add a little more power to this escape, you can try stepping forward as you push the attacker's arm down. As you are pushing the attacker's arm forward and down with your left hand, try stepping towards the attacker with your left leg. This step will add a lot of power to the push because it will help you to use all of your body weight in forcing him down.

SUMMARY

N.B. This summary assumes that the attacker is holding you with his right hand.

1. Move your right hand over the top of the attacker's right hand and place your thumb into the back of his hand. The fingers of your right hand should be in the crease of your attacker's right wrist (palm side of his wrist).

2. Using the heel of your left hand, strike hard into the attacker's right elbow. Keep your left hand applied to the attacker's right elbow on completion of the strike.

3. Two movements: turn your right hand in a clockwise direction; push hard with your right thumb into the back of the attacker's hand.

4. Push on the attacker's right elbow with your left hand, pushing it across your body and downwards.

5. (Optional) Add a further strike if necessary.

6. *Run.*

CONCLUSION

You may have had some difficulty in mastering the wrist and arm locks and, if you did, I promise you that your perseverance will be well rewarded. If you couldn't quite master them, then you've missed something. Go back to the beginning of the section and start again. *Don't* go any further into the book until you have mastered these locks. They are going to be used time and again to get you out of trouble. You must get them right.

As with any escape technique, you can begin by using a shock or stun, to help loosen the attacker's grip. It is up to you. When I explained the arm and wrist lock combined, I mentioned that the elbow was not a very strong joint. Bear this in mind for the future. You may well find that an attacker holding you with either of his arms could be open to a strike to his elbows. If you have ever knocked or bumped your elbow, you will know how painful it is, so I am sure that you can understand just how painful a broken elbow would be.

When you practise the strike to the attacker's elbow, *do not,* under any circumstances, make contact with your partner's elbow. If you strike with any force, you will, at the very least, cause your partner considerable pain. It is more likely, however, that you will break your partner's elbow. So take great care when you practise.

10 Up Against The Wall

In a serious attack situation, a man can hold his victim against a wall, using the wall as a third arm. He can lean on his victim, pinning her to the wall, and use both of his hands to remove his and the victim's clothing. In like manner, he is just as likely to pin his victim to the wall and use only one hand to hold her. His free hand would then be used to remove clothing. A victim can be pinned either with her back or her face to the wall. In either case, a woman held in this fashion can be sure of one thing, she *is* going to be raped if she doesn't escape. Once an attack has got to this stage, the attacker is not going to stop. The only way a woman can hope to get out of trouble now is to pray that help comes or to get out of it herself. Prayer can very often be a great comfort, but sadly may not bring help exactly when you need it. So the only real answer, is to get out of it yourself!

Wall Hold Escape

Let us start with a very common type of wall hold. Look at Figure 76. The attacker is holding the victim into the wall with his body. His hands are free, trying to remove the victim's clothing. This really is a very serious type of attack. The victim has got to be quick and effective. One thing she can't do is to move backwards because the wall stops her. She can't move forward either because the attacker is stopping her. So what *can* she do?

In this situation, the victim has got to be as harsh as the attacker. She *must* shock or stun him. She has many options open to her. Let's assume that she has used the heels of her hands to strike his ears. This striking method, will shock and stun the attacker and will give the victim enough time to escape fully from the hold.

Now look at Figure 77. The victim has done two things. She has placed her left hand onto the right side of

76

the attacker's head and she has moved her left leg diagonally across her body and placed it down slightly behind the attacker's left leg.

Now look at Figure 78. The victim is throwing the attacker to the floor. She is pushing the attacker's head with her left hand and pulling the attacker's left leg with her left leg.

77

78

HOW TO PRACTISE

Start by getting your partner to hold you into a wall in the same way as the attacker is holding the victim in Figure 76. Your partner should have his/her hands near to your hips, as though trying to remove your clothing. Now, you have to start with a shock or stun method. Choose any method you like; knee, elbow, the heels of your hands or a hard stamp onto his toes – anything you like. Just go through the motions of it. Don't hurt your partner. Assuming that you have shocked/stunned the attacker, move your left leg diagonally across your body and place your left foot slightly behind the attacker's left leg. As you make this leg movement, place your left hand onto the right side of the attacker's face. Figure 77 shows the correct position of your leg and hand. Practise that a few times until you feel you have it right. From the position shown in Figure 77, you should pull on the attacker's left leg with your left leg. As you are pulling

on the attacker's left leg, *push* with your left hand, which is on the right side of his face. Your left hand pushes his face across your body, from left to right. Figure 78 shows the outcome of these pushing and pulling movements: the attacker is on the way to the floor.

The correct position is shown in Figure 77. Your left leg and left hand move at the same time. Practise it until you get it right. This throwing technique can be used to escape from many different types of wall hold, so work on it until you can do it with your eyes closed.

It is very important to understand that this throwing method can only be used successfully if the attacker's legs are very close to your own. If the attacker's legs were further away from yours, then you would obviously have to use a different escape method.

SUMMARY

N.B. This summary assumes that you use your left arm and leg to effect the escape.

1. Shock/stun the attacker.

2. Two movements: move your left leg diagonally across your body and place your left foot behind the attacker's left foot; place your left hand onto the right side of the attacker's face.

3. Push the attacker's face/head across your body from your left to right.

4. Pull your left leg back towards your body from your right to left.

5. *Run.*

Wall Hold (Strangle) Escape

By far the most serious unarmed wall hold is the strangle. The reason for its seriousness is simple; the attacker is trying to kill you, not rape you. Having a wall behind you helps the attacker to apply more pressure to your trachea (windpipe). So, should the wall make escaping far more difficult? To the layman it might, but not to us. We are going to use the wall as an ally, not an enemy.

Look at Figure 79. The attacker is using a straight arm strangle. Can you think of any methods you could use to escape from this seemingly very dangerous situation?

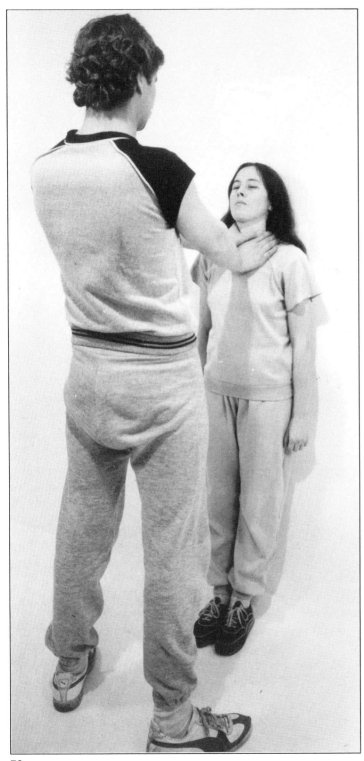

79

80

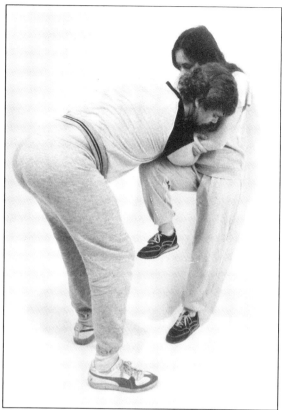

81

Think back to the strangles in Chapter 6. Is there any difference in the way the strangle is applied? (Apart from the wall). Of course not. The application is almost exactly the same, but there are some slight differences. Because the victim has a wall behind her, this means that the attacker can exert a lot more pressure into the actual strangle. This being the case, then the first thing the victim must do is to release the pressure on her throat. As the attacker has both of his arms straight, the victim would probably use a strike to his elbows. The heels of the hand could possibly break the attacker's elbows, or striking with her forearms would do just as well. As soon as the pressure on her throat has been removed, she could then use one of the escape methods described in Chapter 6. Or, she may choose to use the wall to work for her in the following way.

Look at Figure 80. After striking hard at the attacker's elbows, the victim has folded her arms across the top of the attacker's arms.

Now look at Figure 81. The victim has leaned forward and forced the attacker down onto her waiting knee strike.

HOW TO PRACTISE

Before you begin practising the escape method just described, get your partner to apply a strangle hold, while your back is to the wall. Then practise escaping from it by using the methods described in Chapter 6. Practise both the straight arm, and bent arm escape methods. You will find that many of them work just as well from the wall.

Assuming that you have used a strike to the attacker's elbows, fold your arms across the top of the attacker's arms. Figure 80 shows the correct position. Make certain that your elbows are resting above the attacker's elbows. Now, in order to get the attacker down, push your elbows downward. You should push your elbows down as though you were bringing them into your stomach. Your elbows are pulling the attacker's elbows into your body. As you are doing this, push your bottom into the wall. This will have the effect of making you lean slightly forward. Leaning forward adds to your power and therefore makes it easier to get the attacker down. The attacker should be forced to lean into your body and down. Figure 81 shows the position that the attacker should be in. As the attacker is being forced down, your knee can be used to its best advantage, just as it is in the photograph. A strike to the attacker's solar plexus will cause him severe injury. So don't strike your partner, just go through the motions of the knee strike without making contact. Make a mental note of the effect of pushing your bottom into the wall. It causes you to lean forward slightly. Remember this because it will be used in a later escape method.

If you practised the escape methods described in Chapter 6, you should now know several ways of escaping from a strangle against the wall.

SUMMARY
1. Strike the attacker's elbow with both of your forearms.
2. Fold both of your forearms across the attacker's elbows.
3. Push your bottom into the wall and pull the attacker's elbows towards your body.
4. Strike to the attacker's solar plexus with one of your knees.
5. *Run.*

Wall Hold (Single Arm) Escape

Look at Figure 82. The attacker is holding the victim with his right hand and trying to remove her clothing with his left. There are many possible methods which the victim could use to escape from this hold. Can *you* think of any? Think about the escape methods you have already used in past chapters. You could use a wrist or arm lock to dispose of his right hand. His right arm is straight, very vulnerable to injury. The victim has both

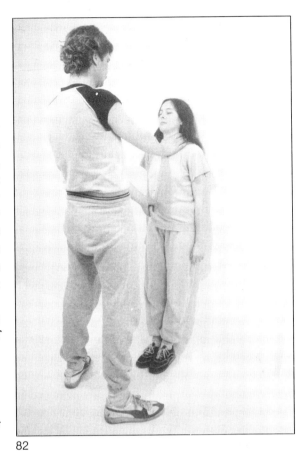

82

of her arms free, so the list of possibilities is endless. The victim could use one of the strangle escape methods if she wanted to. Just because the attacker is holding the victim with only one hand doesn't mean that the victim cannot use the arm-over method of escape. Do you remember the arm-over method? Arm over the attacker's arms and strike back into his head/face with an elbow strike.

HOW TO PRACTISE
This attack is a sort of exercise for you. Get your partner to hold you against the wall as in the photograph. Now, *you* think for yourself. *You* decide how to escape. All you have to do is to think back. Think about the escape methods you have already used; several of them will get you free. If you are going to shock/stun the attacker, be careful.

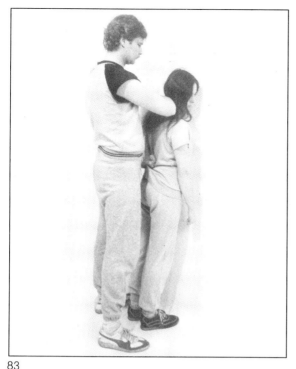

83

84

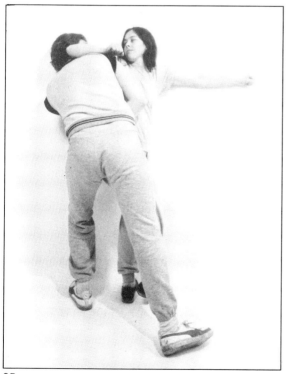

85

Wall Hold (Facing The Wall) Escape No. 1

The most frightening way to be held against a wall is so that you are facing it (Figure 83). To escape from this type of hold is made difficult because the human body is designed to work from the front not the back. Try and eat a meal behind your back. You'll soon see what I mean! The victim can't move backwards or forwards. That leaves only one direction – sidewards.

Look at Figure 84. The attacker is holding the victim into the wall with his right arm and is trying to remove her clothing with his left hand. The victim has moved her left arm out to the side of her body. Her arm is moving in a large circle.

Now look at Figure 85. The victim has moved her arm in a complete circle and has escaped from the hold. She has also used an elbow strike to the attacker's head. She chose this strike because it flowed naturally with the movement of her left arm.

HOW TO PRACTISE

Get your partner to hold you facing against a wall as in Figure 83 by leaning into your back with his right arm. Your partner *must* apply some pressure into your back. Start gently at first; just a little pressure to begin with. You can build up as you get better. Now, with your partner holding you into the wall, clench your left fist. With your left fist clenched beside you, move your left arm in a full circle above your head and back to where it started. Keep your arm straight and keep it close to the wall as it moves in the *full* circle. As you are moving your arm in a circle, twist your hips clockwise. Twisting your hips clockwise should roll your body away from the wall. Practise that a few times; *arm* in a *full* circle and *hips* twist clockwise. When you have that part right, you can add the finishing touches.

As you are twisting your hips, raise your right elbow to your partner's head and *gently* go through the motions of an elbow strike to the head. Your left arm moving in a circle, your hips twisting clockwise and your right elbow moving into the attacker's head, should be done as *one* movement. Practise it as *one* movement and gradually build up your speed and the amount of pressure your partner uses. If you are using your left arm for the circle, your head should look to the right and *vice versa*. This will prevent you from scratching your face on the wall and help you to spin out of the hold much more quickly. As you build up your speed, be very careful with the elbow strike. The force of this strike could easily knock your partner unconscious.

SUMMARY

N.B. This summary assumes that you begin the escape with your left arm.

1. Turn your head and look to the right.

2. Two movements: throw your left arm in a full circle above your head; twist your hips clockwise.

3. Strike into the attacker's head/face with your right elbow.

4. *Run.*

Wall Hold (Facing The Wall) Escape No. 2

An alternative method of escaping from this type of hold is to make a gap between your tummy and the wall.

Assuming that the attacker is holding the victim face against the wall with his arm in her back (Figure 83). What the victim must do next, is to push her knees into the wall. Look at Figure 86. This shows the correct position of the victim's knees. As the victim pushed her knees into the wall, she also pushed her bottom away from the wall. These two movements (knees and bottom) have created a gap between the victim's tummy and the wall. The victim now clenches her left fist and throws a punch between the wall and her tummy. The punch travels through the gap she has created. As she punches, she also twists her hips clockwise, just as she did in the previous escape. The outcome is exactly the same as the previous attack. The victim also uses an elbow strike to complete the escape (Figure 85).

HOW TO PRACTISE

Get your partner to hold you face against the wall with his arm pushing into your back as in Figure 83. Your partner should apply a little pressure to begin with and build it up as you progress. Now look at Figure 86 and push your knees into the wall in the same way as the victim. As you push your knees into the wall, also push your bottom backwards so that it moves into the attacker. You should now be in the same position as the victim in the photograph.

The next part of this escape is very fast. Clench your left fist. Then, throw a punch between your tummy and the wall. Punch as fast and as hard as you possibly can. You are not punching to any target. The punch is to spin your body. Make sure you spin your hips clockwise as you punch. Practise that part of the escape a few times until you get the feel of it. Once you are getting it right, you can add the rest.

This time, when you punch, bring your right elbow up, ready for the strike to the attacker's head. Go through the whole of the escape as though it was only *one* movement: knees and bottom first, then punch, twist your hips and elbow strike all at the same time. If

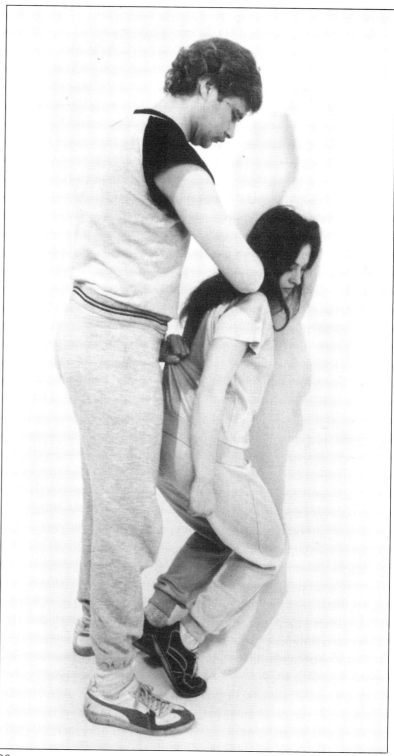

86

you are punching with your left hand, then turn your head to the right before you punch and *vice versa.*

This escape method should be done very quickly. The faster you spin, the more effective the escape and the elbow strike become. In view of the speed of this escape method, you will have to exercise great caution when you practise. An elbow strike done in this manner could easily knock your partner unconscious, so be very careful.

SUMMARY

N.B. This summary assumes that you are going to twist clockwise to effect the escape.

1. Two movements: push your knees into the wall; push your bottom backwards away from the wall.

2. Two movements: use your left hand to throw a punch through the gap between your tummy and the wall; twist your body clockwise.

3. Strike into the attacker's head/face with your right elbow.

4. *Run.*

CONCLUSION

Some of the wall escapes you have been shown are also used and taught to various members of the Armed Forces. This in itself shows how effective these escape methods are.

Some of the wall escape methods have to be used with a strike to the attacker. If you are worried by this, then ask yourself a question: 'would he have worried about me, or my family, if his *rape* attempt had succeeded?'

If you are being held against a wall, then you are being forced against your will to do something you don't want to do. The attacker is using violence against *you.* Once he has removed your clothes, do you really think he's going to stop? Do you really think he gives a jot about you or what he's putting you through?

Though I never condone the use of violence, I do realise that there are times when, in order to end violence, one has to use violence. If attacked and pinned against a wall, I believe that this is just such a time.

11 Pulling Attacks

Woman who are attacked out of doors, in a park or on the street, are very often pulled by the attacker to somewhere out of view of the Public. The most common way a woman can expect to be pulled by an attacker, is by one or both wrists. So these are the first attacks I shall deal with.

Two Arm Pulling Escape No. 1

Look at Figure 87. The attacker is holding the victim's wrists and is trying to pull her forward (towards him) to somewhere out of view. The victim is naturally resisting him, but in a rather special way (I shall explain later) so

88

that she can use *his* strength to effect an escape and injure the attacker into the bargain. This type of attack can only be described as very dangerous. If the attacker successfully pulls you out of view, then make no mistake; he is going to *rape* and probably injure or even kill you. Why else does he want to pull you out of sight?

Now look at Figure 88. The victim has moved forward and used her right leg as a pivot. Using her right leg as a pivot, she was able to deliver a maximum power knee strike into the attacker's groin. The victim could have delivered the strike to other parts of the attacker's body, such as the solar plexus or stomach, but she chose his groin as a matter of course. Obviously, the victim would push the attacker away from her as soon as the strike was delivered, and then *run* to get help, if not for herself, then for the attacker.

HOW TO PRACTISE

This escape method is very, very dangerous for the attacker. It would be very easy to maim or even kill a would-be attacker with this escape method. I have only included it in this book in case you stumbled across it by chance. If the dangers of this escape are explained, then at least you shouldn't get carried away when you practise. It is much safer for you to understand how dangerous it is, rather than have you practise it without realising the dangers involved.

Look at Figure 87. The attacker is pulling the victim by the wrists. Look closely at the victim's position. Her left leg is bent. Her right leg is straight. She has bent her left leg as much as possible and in doing so, her body weight has dropped. She has lowered her body weight as close to the floor as possible. Her right leg is straight to make it more difficult for the attacker to pull her forward. It is straight for a second reason: it is going to act as a pivot for her left knee.

Now get your partner to hold your wrists and position yourself exactly as the victim in the photograph. Get your partner to pull you slightly forward. As your partner pulls you forward, concentrate on keeping your right leg straight and resist. Keep your right heel planted firmly into the floor. Bend your left leg as far as it will go, so that your bottom is almost on the floor. If you get it right, your partner will find it difficult to pull you forward. Practise that for a short time. When you can feel it becoming difficult for your partner to pull you, then you will know you are getting it right. When you feel that you have that part right, you can add the rest of the escape.

The rest of this escape is very, very dangerous for the attacker. You *must* take great care when you practise. Do it slowly and gently. Take your time. If you overdo it, you *will* seriously injure your partner. I cannot stress strongly enough the importance of doing this part of the escape very slowly. Please heed my warning!

The next part of the escape uses your straight right leg as a pivot and your left bent leg as a coiled spring. Get your partner to pull you forward, just as before. But now, as you resist, *gently* push yourself forward with your left bent leg. As you are pushing yourself forward, your right leg remains straight. It acts as a pivot and a stabiliser. Practise that a few times until you get the feel of it. When you have progressed that far, you can complete the escape.

Look at Figure 88 which shows the final part of the escape. As you are using your left bent leg as a spring to push you forward, you simply raise the same leg in front of you and complete the escape with a very powerful knee strike. It doesn't matter where you hit the attacker, because the force of the strike is, to say the least, devastating. The reason the knee strike is so powerful is due to a combination of three main factors: firstly, the attacker's strength pulling you forward; secondly, your body moving forward, and finally, the strength and power of your own leg as it drives into the target.

89

SUMMARY

N.B. This summary assumes that you are going to strike the attacker with your left knee.

1. Keep your right leg straight and dig your right heel into the floor.

2. Bend your left leg and lower your body as close to the floor as possible.

3. Use your left leg to push yourself into the attacker.

4. Strike into the attacker's body with your left knee.

5. Push the attacker away from you.

6. *Run.*

Two Arm Pulling Escape No. 2

There are several alternatives that you can use to escape if being pulled by an attacker. You could, if you wanted to, just push the attacker to the floor. This escape method is very similar to the last one, in that it begins in the same way. Figure 87 shows you how to resist an attacker who is pulling you by the wrists.

Now look at Figure 89. The victim resisted the attacker in exactly the same way as before, but this time, instead of using a knee strike, she has simply stepped forward on her left leg and pushed the attacker backwards, causing him to fall down. The victim has pushed the attacker's shoulders. She was able to do this because she surprised him. He was pulling against a strong resistance and then suddenly, the resistance had

gone. This caused him to stumble backwards and momentarily release his grip. The victim made full use of this and immediately pushed hard on his shoulders to help him on his way.

This escape method is much safer for the attacker because any injuries he gets will be caused by his falling to the floor. As soon as the attacker falls down, the victim gains those extra seconds she needs to get help. As always, she *runs!*

HOW TO PRACTISE

This escape method starts in the same way as the first one. Get your partner to pull you by the wrists. You resist the pulling as you did before by adopting the resistance stance shown in Figure 87. Now, using your left bent leg as a coiled spring, step forward as fast as you can. Just do that part a few times. Your partner should stumble backwards if he/she is pulling hard. When you feel you are getting the step forward correct, you can add the finishing touches.

This time, as you step forward on your left leg, use

your arms to pull yourself forward. The attacker will have a tight grip on your wrists, so pulling yourself forward should be very easy. You *step* and *pull* at the same time. Using your arms to pull yourself forward will increase your forward momentum very considerably, thus adding to the force you use to push the attacker down. As you are moving forward, you will find that your arms bend slightly, so place your hands onto the attacker's shoulders and use them to push him backwards.

All of these small points help to increase the force with which you push the attacker backwards. The harder you push him, the further away he will go.

Be very careful when you practise this escape method and make sure there are no obstacles behind your partner when you push him/her. It is best to practise this escape method in a garden, or at least somewhere with a soft landing.

This escape method works best when the attacker pulls really hard. The harder he pulls, the further he travels. On one occasion, when practising this escape method, one of my instructors travelled some 20 feet before he hit the wall. He dislocated his shoulder on impact and needed hospital treatment to repair the damage!

There are many variations you can use for escaping from this type of attack. The important part of the escape is the resistance stance shown in Figure 87. Practise this part of the escape regularly. When you feel absolutely confident that you have it right, you can vary the second, pushing, part of the escape to suit yourself.

You may like to step forward and, instead of just pushing or using a knee strike to the attacker, you may like to use a front kick. If you want to use a front kick, you should find that the attacker's knee is an easy target or, if you have been practising the leg techniques regularly, you may find that you can use a front kick to the attacker's chest. The choice is yours. Whether you use a strike or not, isn't important. The important thing is to escape and get help.

SUMMARY
This summary assumes that you are going to step forward onto your left leg to effect the escape.
1. Adopt the *resistance stance* as you did previously: right leg straight, left leg bent, body close to the floor.
2. Two movements: pull yourself forward with both of your arms; step forward with your left leg.
3. Push the attacker's shoulders with both of your hands.
4. *Run.*

Single Arm Pulling Escape

As well as holding both of your wrists when he pulls you, an attacker is just as likely to hold only one of your wrists and this presents us with a slightly different problem. Once he starts to pull you, the effect is such that it will turn you sidewards to the attacker.

Look at Figure 90. The attacker has pulled the victim's right arm and, in doing so, the victim has been turned sideways on the attacker. So, in order to escape, the victim has to use a similar type of resistance stance.

Look at Figure 91. The victim has adopted a sideways resistance stance. Her right leg is straight and her left leg is bent. This stance is very similar to the frontal resistance stance. The main difference, of course, is that the victim is sideways on to the attacker. The victim has lowered her body weight by bending her left leg. In dropping her body weight, the victim has made it much more difficult for the attacker to pull her out of view. Her right leg acts as a stop as well as a pivot and again this makes it more difficult for the attacker to pull her out of view.

Now look at Figure 92. The victim has, after resisting, moved immediately into a step through side kick and delivered it into the attacker's stomach. The victim used the same principle of resist and release as she did before to surprise the attacker. The victim could have delivered the strike to the attacker's knee had she wanted to, but she had been practising the leg techniques regularly and decided to strike to the attacker's stomach instead!

90

91

HOW TO PRACTISE

Start by facing your partner. Now get your partner to grip your right wrist and pull you as hard as possible. You will find that your body turns sideways to your partner. Once you have been turned sideways by your partner, sink immediately into the sideways resistance stance, as shown in Figure 91. The next part of this escape method is very much the same as the previous one. First of all, you resist the attacker. Then, when you're ready, move into the step through side kick. You should kick with your right leg, because it is the leg closest to the attacker.

92

As with the previous escape method, you can use the arm that is being held to pull yourself into the attacker.

When you are practising, concentrate on getting the resistance stance correct. Figure 91 shows the correct position. Start slowly and gently and, above all, be careful *not* to hit your partner with the step through side kick. As you practise this escape method, you may find that you can use many different striking methods. You may even prefer not to strike at all. No matter whether you strike or not, the most important part of this escape is the resistance stance. Practise until it is correct every time and then you can catch the attacker offguard.

This escape method and the first one are very similar, so you will probably be able to mix the pushing parts of the escapes to suit yourself. For example, you may find that you can use a front kick when you are pulled from the side. Similarly, you may find that you can use a side kick when you are pulled from the front. Practise it and discover for yourself which striking methods complement you best. Many women find that, when they are pulled from the side, they can step forward and push the attacker backwards, just as they did when they were being pulled from the front. It is up to you to decide what is suitable for yourself.

Practise hard because, out on the streets, you won't have time to find out which methods suit you best. Fore-warned is forearmed!

SUMMARY

N.B. This summary assumes that you are being pulled by your right arm.

1. Keep your right leg straight and dig your right heel into the floor.

2. Bend your left leg and lower your body as close to the floor as possible.

3. Use your right hand to pull yourself into the attacker.

4. Execute a step through side kick into the attacker's body.

5. *Run.*

Pulling By The Feet Escape

What do you think would happen if, for some reason, the attacker were to release his grip as he was trying to pull you? The answer is simple. It would be *you* that ended up on the floor. Now, let us suppose that the attacker still wants to *rape* you. You would be on the floor and the attacker would be standing. He still has to get you out of view to commit the crime. The chances are that your feet would be the nearest part of your body to him.

Look at Figure 93. The victim has fallen to the floor and the attacker has gripped both of her feet and is pulling her out of view. I could almost feel sorry for this attacker because he doesn't know what's going to happen to him next.

Look at Figure 94. The victim has pulled herself towards the attacker. She has done this by pulling her knees up to her chest. Her hands have gripped the attacker's ankles.

Now look at Figure 95. The victim has pushed the attacker with both of her feet. She pushed him as though she were kicking him. She kicked to his stomach or chest and, as she kicked, she held on tightly to his ankles. Because the attacker's ankles were held tightly, he fell down. The victim is still holding the attacker's ankles and this keeps him down. The victim's feet are poised, ready to strike to the attacker's groin. As soon as she has delivered the strike to his groin, she runs to get help. Even though the attacker probably can't run, she can – and does. Discretion is always the better part of valour!

HOW TO PRACTISE

It's best to practise this escape method with your husband or boyfriend because this method works best with a strong attacker. The stronger the attacker, the better it works.

Look at Figure 93. Get your partner to hold your feet or ankles, as the attacker is holding the victim in the photograph.

Now look at Figure 94. As your partner pulls you along the floor, raise your knees to your chest. As you are raising your knees, keep your arms by your sides.

Then, when your knees reach your chest, *firmly grip* the attacker's ankles. Practice that part of the escape a few times. Be careful when you grip your partner's ankles. The next part of the escape will put the attacker on the floor. All you have to do now is push hard with both of your feet as though you were kicking. Push into the attacker's stomach or chest and keep tight hold of his ankles as you push/kick.

When you have pushed/kicked, the attacker will fall to the floor as in Figure 95. Once you are in this position, you should still be holding his ankles. You have now reversed the roles. It is the attacker who is at your mercy; he is on the floor with his legs slightly apart and your

feet are poised, ready to strike the most vulnerable part of his body.

You may find, when you are practising this escape method, that just by pulling your knees hard into your chest, the attacker will release his grip. If he does, then you must get up quickly. Get up and *run*. The whole point of this escape method, is to get the attacker onto the floor in a vulnerable position. If you raise your knees too quickly and the attacker *does* release his grip, then you have to hope that the attacker is really stupid and tries to do the same thing again. He may well oblige you, but it's very doubtful. If he's failed once, he'll more than likely try something different. So practise and get it

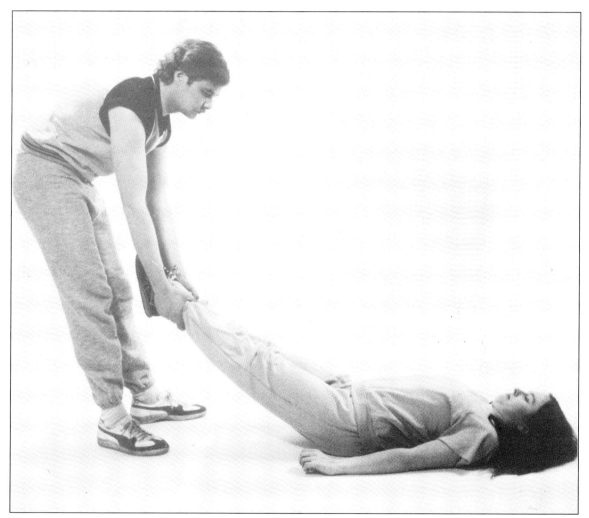

93

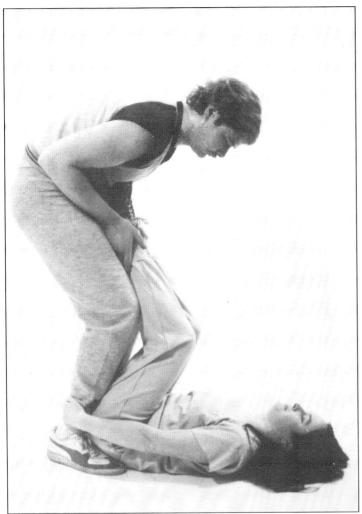

94

95

right. Raise your knees too quickly and you still have a problem. Get it right and the attacker has a problem.

This escape method will work well, even if the attacker holds only one of your feet or ankles. The only difference is that you will probably only be able to grip *one* of his ankles. If you can grip both, then that's fine. But if you can only grip *one*, just go through the same movements as before. Practise it. Get your partner to pull only one of your ankles and go through the escape method, just as you did before.

A final safety precaution when practising this escape method is to make sure your partner has got a soft landing and don't push/kick too hard.

SUMMARY
1. Pull your knees up to your chest.
2. Grip both of the attacker's ankles with your hands.
3. Keep tight hold of the attacker's ankles and push hard into his stomach with both of your feet.
4. (Optional) The attacker will now be on the floor with his legs apart. You will still be holding his ankles. Raise one or both of your knees up to your chest and strike into his groin with your foot/feet.
5. Get up and *run*.

Pulling Along The Floor Escape

Suppose you were to be in a resistance stance and, for some reason, you tripped or slipped over. What do you think would happen?

The attacker would still be trying to pull you out of view and you would be getting dragged along the floor, still held by your wrists as in Figure 96. It looks almost hopeless. The victim is in a very vulnerable position. Well, vulnerable or not, she can still escape.

Look at Figure 97. The victim has twisted the attacker's arms so that they are crossing over themselves. The attacker's arms have almost been tied into a knot. The victim did this by simply rotating her body clockwise through a full 360° turn.

Now look at Figure 98. The victim has continued turning her body clockwise and has really tied up the attacker's arms. She has shocked the attacker by doing this and, as a result of shocking him, has been able to stand up. She could, if she wanted to, use a striking method to stun the attacker. It is up to her. The important thing is that she has escaped from what seemed a hopeless position. In so doing, she has gained extra time to escape and get help.

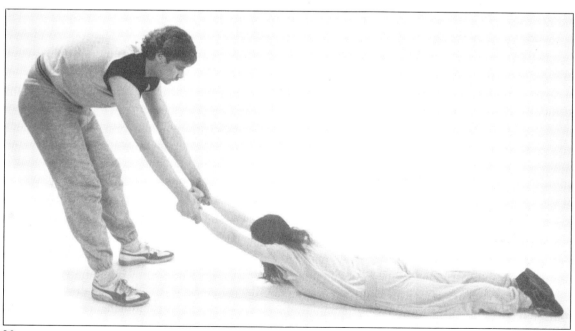

97

98

HOW TO PRACTISE

Start by lying face down on the floor, just as the victim is doing in Figure 96. Now, without your partner pulling you, just roll over onto your back and, as you are rolling over, grip your partner's wrists with your hands. Roll over clockwise so that you can follow the step-by-step photographs. Once you have mastered the technique, you can roll over in any direction. Practise that part first: just roll over clockwise onto your back and grip your partner's wrists tightly. When you have that part right, get your partner to pull you as you roll over.

Try that a few times, then add the next part. Now, as your partner is pulling you, roll over, grip his wrists and continue rolling through a full 360°, so that you end up face down again. Your partner's arms will be twisted around themselves because you are using the whole of your body weight to twist and he is only using the strength in his arms to hold you.

Figure 97 shows the position you should now be in. Check your own position with the photograph. If you are not in the same position, then you have done something wrong. Try it again until you get it right. When you are positioning yourself as in the photograph, you can add the rest.

When you are practising the clockwise roll, get your partner to *stop* pulling you as you complete the full 360° turn. Now, practise the end of the escape, but *without* your partner pulling you. You are in the position shown in Figure 97. Now continue to roll, still holding your partner's wrists. Just roll onto your right side. As you continue to roll onto your right side, pull yourself towards your partner with your arms. As you are pulling yourself towards your partner, raise your right knee up to your chest. Stay on your side. You should be able to kneel on your right knee quite easily from here. Then you simply stand up on your left leg.

It may sound complicated, but it is much easier than it sounds. I will condense the second part of the escape for you. From the position shown in Figure 97, continue to roll onto your right side. As you continue to roll, pull yourself towards your partner and raise your right knee into your chest. You are now on your right side with your right knee raised up to your chest. From this position simply kneel onto your right knee. Once

kneeling on your right knee, stand up. Then the rest is up to you.

When you have the second part of the escape right, *without* your partner pulling, get your partner to pull you and then go through the second part exactly as I have described. Remember to start as shown in Figure 97. You will find it much easier to escape when your partner *is* pulling you. Your forward motion will help you to roll more easily and help you to stand up much easier as well.

When you have practised both parts of the escape with your partner pulling you, all you have to do is put both parts together and practise the whole thing. You will find that the faster you roll, the easier it is to stand up. Once you are standing, you will have the attacker's arms tied up. So, if you want, you could add a knee strike or something similar to finish the escape. That part is up to you. You decide! Just a word of warning; if, when you are rolling, you fail to grip the attackers wrist's, and continue to roll, the attacker will be forced to release *his* grip on you. In releasing *his* grip, you will be free from the immediate danger of *his* pulling attack, but you will still be on the floor and *he* will be standing. In this case, you must move *fast. Don't* wait around trying to figure out what went wrong, *run!* If he runs after you, you can still floor him by using the running escape methods you practised previously.

If you were to be pulled along the ground by only *one* of your arms, you would escape using the same method but you would use *both* of your hands to grip the attacker's offending wrist. You wouldn't tie *both* of his arms in a knot, but you would apply a terrific arm and wrist lock. Try it for yourself. Get your partner to pull you along the ground by only *one* of your arms and, as he is pulling you, use the same escape method but grip his offending wrist with *both* your hands and keep rolling. Don't let him go. Discover what happens for yourself, because that is what this book is all about, finding out what complements *you* best. Experiment for yourself. You will be amazed at the outcome!

SUMMARY

N.B. This summary assumes that you are going to roll in a clockwise direction in order to effect the escape.

1. Two movements: roll over clockwise onto your back; grip the attacker's wrists with both of your hands.

2. Keeping hold of the attacker's wrists, continue rolling clockwise so that you are face down on the floor.

3. Two movements: continue rolling clockwise just enough to get you onto your right side; use your arms to pull yourself towards the attacker.

4. Two movements: raise your right knee up to your chest; kneel onto your right knee.

5. Stand up. Keep a firm grip of the attacker's wrists when you stand.

6. (Optional) Add a knee strike or leg strike to complete the escape.

7. *Run.*

CONCLUSION

This chapter has described some *very severe* striking methods. It is important for you to know that, if you use them, then, at the very least, you can *seriously* injure an attacker. Maybe even worse . . . The only reason I have included them in this book is to safeguard *you*. If I had left them out, then it is very possible that you would have discovered them for yourself. In discovering them for yourself, you may have practised them and, ignorant of the danger, injured your partner.

If you were to be attacked in the way I've described, then it would be up to you to decide how to escape. Knowing how dangerous these striking methods are, should help you to make up your mind.

You should find, as you practise escaping from this kind of attack, that many of the escape methods described in previous chapters will also get you free. For instance, if an attacker were to hold only one of your arms and then start pulling you, could you use one of the arm hold escape methods to get free? Try it. If you have practised the arm hold escapes, you should be able to combine the resistance stance with an arm hold escape method. Similarly, if an attacker were to hold your clothing near your neck and then start to pull you, you should find that one of the strangle escape methods combined with the resistance stance will also get you free. You must try it for yourself. You must find what works best for you, *before* you get attacked. It is no good locking the gate after the horse has bolted!

12 On The Floor

Many attackers will try to pin you to the floor. Once an attacker has managed to get you down, then this is your very last chance to escape. Make no mistake, once an attacker has you in this position, you really have no alternative but to shock and stun him. He is not going to let you go now. He has probably been struggling with you before he managed to get you onto the floor and everything you have tried so far has failed. No matter what the reason, whether you haven't practised enough, or you haven't read the book properly, you are in a very dangerous situation. You are going to be raped if you don't escape now. This is your last chance. Fail now and you will have an horrific memory to carry with you for the rest of your life. An attacker who pins you to the floor will normally hold you with only one arm and try to remove your clothing with his free hand. It is just as possible that he will straddle you. If he does straddle you, then he will more than likely try to trap your arms beneath his legs. If he's a beginner at rape, then he may straddle you and leave your arms free. No matter how he pins you down, you have to make sure that your reaction will count. So practise the escapes in this chapter as though your life depends on it because one day it could.

Floor Escape No. 1

Look at Figure 99. The attacker is holding the victim down with his right arm and is trying to remove her clothing with his left hand. In order to keep her down, he has to lean hard onto his right arm. This is his mistake. He is concentrating on two things. Firstly, he has to keep her pinned to the floor. Secondly, he has to remove her clothing to commit his crime. As most of his body weight is on his right arm and there is almost no weight at all on his left, we can use this knowledge to effect an escape. Both of the victim's arms are free and she can still use her legs and feet to escape. Look closely at Figure 99. You can see that the victim would have no difficulty in kicking to the attacker's head if she wanted to. If the victim chose to kick to the attacker's head, she would use her right leg for the strike because it has the clearest path to the target. In kicking the attacker's head, she would not only shock and stun him, she would more probably seriously injure or even kill him. Let's assume that the victim doesn't want to run the risk of kicking the attacker's head.

Look at Figure 100. The victim has taken her left hand over the top of the attacker's right hand. She has placed her thumb into the back of the attacker's hand and placed her fingers into the attacker's wrist, on the palm side of his hand. This is the first position of the wrist lock.

Now look at Figure 101. The victim has rolled her left hand in an anti-clockwise direction. She has also applied her right hand to the attacker's right hand. She is now using both of her hands to effect the wrist lock. (Notice the victim's right knee. It has been raised and she has planted her right foot firmly into the floor. You'll understand why when you begin to practise).

Now look at Figure 102. The victim has applied a

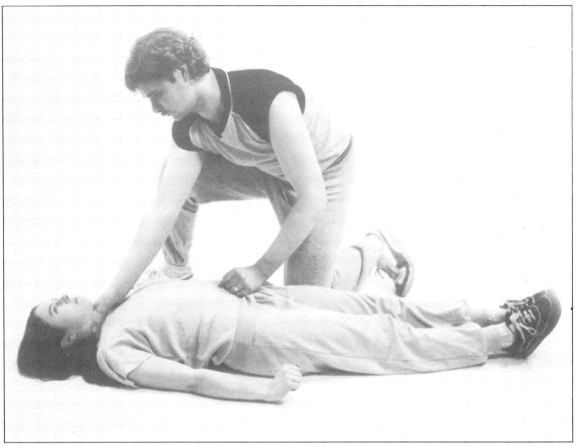

99

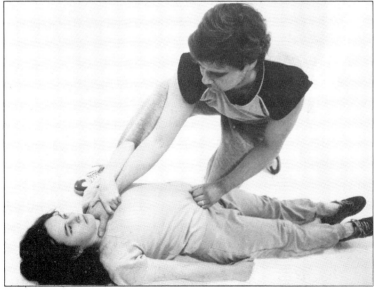

100

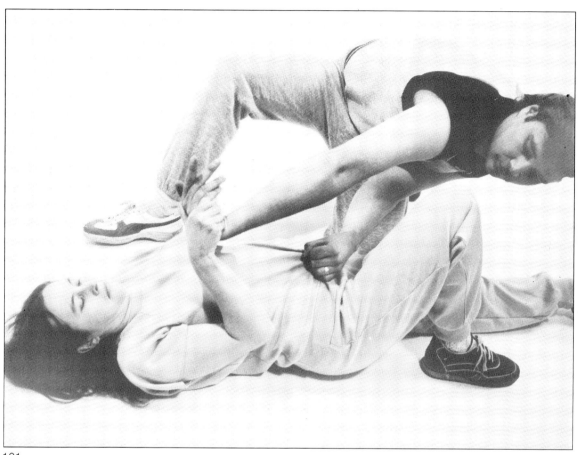

101

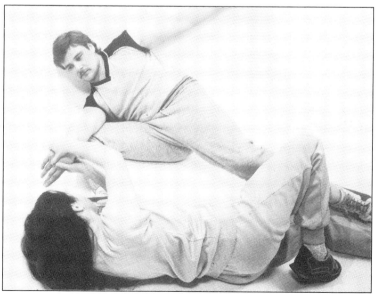

102

wrist lock to the attacker's right hand and is now rolling towards him, forcing him to the floor. Once the attacker has been forced to the floor, the victim will have no trouble standing up. She will stand up very easily because she keeps the wrist lock applied tightly to the attacker's right hand.

HOW TO PRACTISE

Get your partner to hold you down exactly as shown in Figure 99. Later on, you can practise escaping with your partner holding you on the opposite side of your body.

If you want to practise kicking to the attacker's head, then be very careful. *Don't* make contact. Just raise your *right* leg gently and slowly. It doesn't need much practice; you only need to know that it can be done. It is for you to decide whether or not to use this striking method. Having tried the kick to the head, we'll go on to the wrist lock escape method.

Look at Figure 100. Move your left hand over the top of your partner's right hand and place your fingers into your partner's wrist, on the palm side of his/her hand. Place your thumb into the back of your partner's hand, towards the knuckles. Now, using Figure 101 as a guide, raise your right knee and plant your right foot firmly onto the floor. You have raised your right knee in preparation for the completion of the escape. You should now be in the same position as the victim in Figure 101: your left hand applied to the attacker's right hand, right knee raised, right foot planted firmly into the floor.

Using your left hand, twist your attacker's right hand in an anti-clockwise direction and then quickly apply your right hand to the attacker's right hand. Both of your thumbs are into the attacker's wrist. Now you can complete the escape.

Push your thumbs hard into the back of the attacker's hand and keep twisting his hand in an anti-clockwise direction. Keep the attacker's wrist close to your body when you are twisting it. As you are twisting the attacker's wrist, your right foot pushes down hard into the floor and will help you to roll into the attacker's arm (Figure 102). By rolling into the attacker's arm, you will cause him to fall to the floor. The attacker's falling to the floor is a completely involuntary action on his part. The only way he can ease the pain in his wrist is to go down; his body will do it by itself. When the attacker goes down, keep the wrist lock applied with both of your hands and stand up. When you are standing up, the rest is up to you. You will be standing with the wrist lock still applied to the attacker's wrist and he will be on the floor at your mercy. You can decide for yourself whether any further action is necessary.

Practise this escape method until you can do it with your eyes closed. The more you practise the better you will become. It is a waste of time trying this method only once or twice because, in a real attack, you are not going to get a second chance to try it. It's got to work *first* time. Fail now and *you* will be one of the statistics at the beginning of my next book.

SUMMARY

N.B. This summary assumes that the attacker is on the left side of your body.

1. Move your left hand over the top of the attacker's right hand, place your fingers into the crease of your attacker's wrist and place your thumb into the back of his hand toward the knuckle.

2. Raise your right knee and plant your right foot firmly onto the floor.

3. Two movements: twist the attackers right hand in an anti-clockwise direction; apply your right hand to the attacker's right hand so that both of your thumbs are into the back of the attacker's right hand and your fingers in the crease of his wrist on the palm side.

4. Keep twisting his hand anti-clockwise and push your thumbs hard into the back of his hand. Keep his wrist close to your body when you are twisting it.

5. Two movements: push down hard on your right foot; roll your body anti-clockwise. Keep the wrist lock applied.

6. Stand up and keep the wrist lock applied.

7. (Optional) Add a further strike to the attacker's body if you wish.

8. *Run.*

Floor Escape No. 2

Another way in which you can escape from this type of attack, is by using your legs as a pair of scissors. Let's assume that the attacker has applied the same hold to the victim as shown in Figure 99. The victim this time decides to use her legs to escape.

Look at Figure 103. The victim has applied her legs to the attacker's neck; her legs are crossed.

Now look at Figure 104. The victim has rolled her body in a special way and the attacker has been forced to the floor and probably banged his head in the process.

The victim could, if she wanted to, quickly release the scissors hold on the attacker's head or body. I'm *not* suggesting that you should kick the attacker's head or body, merely pointing out the possibilities. Once he has been forced down, he will be shocked and, in being shocked, you should be able to escape from him by *running*.

HOW TO PRACTISE

Get your partner to hold you to the floor, just as the attacker is holding the victim in Figure 99. The attacker

103

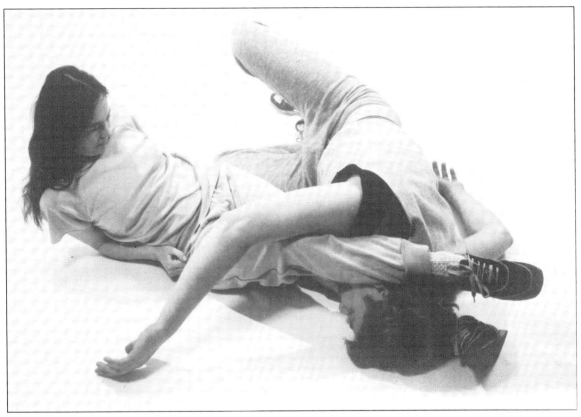

104

should be on your left. Now look at Figure 103. Raise your right leg above your partner's head and gently place it on your partner's neck, exactly as in the photograph. Be very careful not to hit your partner as you raise your leg. As you are raising your right leg, you also raise your left leg and place it gently onto the other side of your partner's neck. Use extreme caution when you practise this combination of leg movements, because the neck is a very vulnerable spot and can be easily damaged. Practise only those two leg movements: right leg above his head and place on the right side of his neck; left leg raised up to the left side of his neck. Once you have that part right, you can go on to the second part of the escape.

The second part of this escape is *extremely dangerous* for the attacker. Once your feet are held in the correct position around the attacker's neck, a harsh movement could break it. So, in the interests of safety while you practise, get your partner to hold his/her neck with both hands. Then, and only then, can you continue with the second part of this escape.

With your feet applied to the attacker's neck, roll your body to the right (clockwise) and, at the same time, straighten your legs and really tense the muscles in them. You should only roll enough to move onto your right hip. As you straighten and tense your legs, your feet should meet behind the attacker's neck and lock tightly. As you roll onto your right hip, the attacker will be forced down to the floor. Once the attacker is on the floor, the rest is up to you. I doubt if he will be much of a threat now, but he may be. So *run*, and get help – if not for you, then for him!

There are a few points to remember when practising this escape method. Firstly, be very careful when you raise your legs to the attacker's neck. If you are raising your right leg *above* the attacker's head, i.e. to the right side of his neck, you will increase your speed considerably if you raise it as though you were kicking.

Try the leg raise: first bending your knee and plant your foot firmly on the floor, then, kick it up as fast as you can. This will have the advantage of using the strength in your foot as well as your hip when you raise your leg. The faster you raise your leg, the quicker you will escape.

Once your feet are applied to the attacker's neck, the important thing to remember is to roll in the direction of the *upper* leg. So, if your right leg is above your left, you roll to the right and *vice versa*. If, for some reason, you were to get your legs mixed up, and you were attacked in the same way as the victim in Figure 99, i.e. with the attacker on your left, you would have your left leg above your right. In this case, you still follow the formula as described. Roll in the direction of the *upper* leg, i.e. to your left. The attacker will still be forced to the floor, but you will end up on your tummy with the neck lock still applied. Try it for yourself. You may even prefer it with your left leg above your right.

In rolling towards the *upper* leg, you will tighten the neck lock, but if you roll away from the upper leg, you will release the lock.

Practise escaping with the attacker applying the hold from both sides of your body, i.e. from the left and right side. In a real attack, you can't ask the attacker to apply the hold from your better side, so be prepared. It's always better to be safe than sorry.

SUMMARY

N.B. This summary assumes that the attacker is on the left side of your body.

1. Two movements: raise your right leg above the attacker's head and place it on the right side of his neck; raise your left leg and place it on the left side of his neck.

2. With your legs applied to your attacker's neck, tense your legs and roll to the right (clockwise). You will be rolling onto your right hip.

3. (Optional) Add a further strike if necessary.

4. *Run.*

Floor Strangle (Arms Free) Escape No. 1

One of the most dangerous situations in which a woman can find herself is when the attacker straddles her and tries to strangle her. Strangulation is one of the most common forms of homicide in Great Britain, so it makes sense to know how to escape from this type of attack. As I mentioned in earlier chapters, a man who tries to strangle you *is* trying to kill you. You have got to escape first time because, if you don't, you are going to die.

Look at Figure 105. The attacker has straddled the victim and is trying to strangle her. The victim's arms are free, so she can use them to assist in her escape.

Now look at Figure 106. The victim has moved her hands into a wrist and arm lock position.

Figure 107 shows the victim escaping by applying a wrist and arm lock. Before the victim effected the escape, she shocked and stunned the attacker. I will explain how in the practice section.

HOW TO PRACTISE

Look at Figure 105. Get your partner to straddle you in the same way that the attacker in the photograph is straddling the victim. Your partner should place his/her hands on your throat, as though strangling you. Once you are in this position, try and see how you can use your hands and arms to shock or stun the attacker. You may find that your hands will reach the attacker's ears. If they do, then you could use the heels of your hands to strike both of his ears, just as you have learned in previous chapters. You should find that you can easily strike to the attacker's elbows, again with the heels of your hands. No matter how you choose to strike, you must make it count, so *you* decide which method is best for *you*. The victim in the photograph used the heel of her right hand to strike hard into the attacker's left elbow. If you decide to use this striking method, then first you should apply your left hand to the attacker's left hand. This will ensure that his elbow takes the full force of the blow.

Now look at Figure 106. As soon as you have used a strike to the attacker's elbow, you should be in the same position as the victim in the photograph. Your left hand

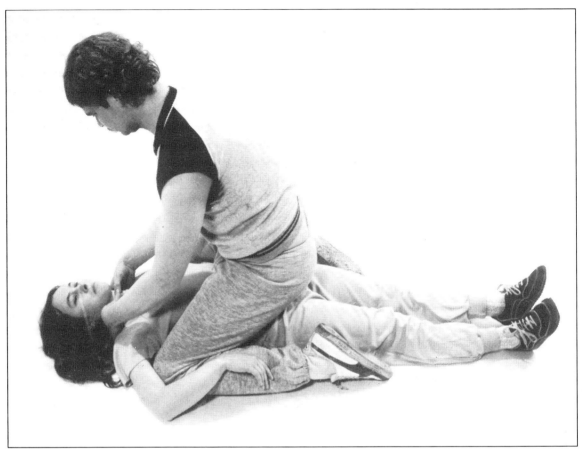

105

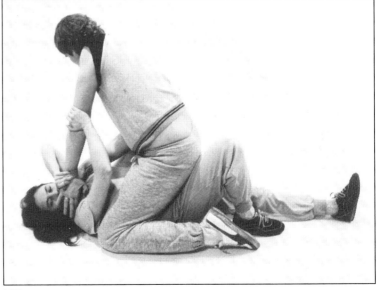

106

is applied to the attacker's left hand, ready for the wrist lock. Your fingers should be on the palm side of the attacker's hand and your thumb should be applied to the back of his hand, close to the knuckle, just as you have done in other escapes. Your right knee should be raised with your right foot planted firmly onto the floor. Your right leg *must* be in the position shown in Figure 106. This is going to increase your strength when you throw the attacker off your body. Practise getting into the correct position a few times. Be careful not to injure your partner when you strike. Just go through the motions of striking and then get into the correct position. When you are getting it right every time you

can complete the escape.

Your left hand twists the attacker's left hand, in an anti-clockwise direction. The thumb of your left hand pushes hard into the back of the attacker's hand.

Your right hand, which is applied to the attacker's left elbow, pushes hard across your body, from right to left.

Your body twists in an anti-clockwise direction. Your right foot, which is planted firmly onto the floor, pushes down hard into the floor. This will help you to twist your body with far more power. This *whole* combination of movements should be done at the same time. Twist his hand, push his elbow and roll your body.

If you look at Figure 107 you can see that the victim

107

has kept the arm and wrist lock applied as she rolled the attacker off her body. In doing this, the victim will have the attacker in a very vulnerable position and, if she wants to, should be able to use a further striking method to stun the attacker. Practise the second part of the escape exactly as described. Make sure that you are in the same position as the victim in Figure 106 before you roll the attacker off your body. Once the attacker has been forced off, try and keep the arm and wrist lock applied and try to stand up. Once you are standing up, you will be in a much better position to get away and get help. If you don't manage to stand up, then you will still have a chance to get away, because the attacker will still be on the floor *shocked* and *stunned*.

SUMMARY

1. Shock/stun the attacker.
2. Apply your left hand to the attacker's left hand ready for the wrist lock, fingers on the palm side of his hand, your thumb in the back of his hand close to the knuckle.
3. Raise your right knee and place your right foot firmly on the floor.
4. Apply your right hand to the attacker's left elbow.
5. Three movements: twist your left hand anti-clockwise and push hard with your thumb into the back of his hand (keep his wrist close to your body as you twist it); push hard into his elbow with your right hand from your right to left; push down hard into the floor with your right foot so that your body rolls anti-clockwise, forcing the attacker onto the floor.
6. Keep the wrist and arm lock applied and stand up.
7. (Optional) Add a further strike if necessary.
8. *Run.*

Floor Strangle (Arms Free) Escape No. 2

From the same attack position shown in Figure 105, there is another escape method which may work even better for you. It employs the same *rolling* technique, but the attacker this time will have two damaged elbows and may even be knocked unconscious.

Look at Figure 108. The victim is being attacked in the same way as before, but this time she has used her forearms to strike the attacker's elbows. She has hit both of the attacker's elbows simultaneously.

Now look at Figure 109. She has rolled the attacker off her body, but she has held the attacker's arms with her forearms and, because she is holding his arms, he can't protect his head from the floor as he goes down. The faster you roll your body in this escape, the harder he will hit his head. As soon as the attacker has been rolled off, the victim would *run!*

You could if you wanted, use the same type of escape but, instead of using your forearms to strike and hold the attacker's elbows, you could use the heels of your hands. In this case, you would hold his elbows with your hands, instead of your forearms as you rolled him off.

HOW TO PRACTISE

Get your partner to straddle you as shown in Figure 105. The first part of the escape is a simultaneous strike with both of your forearms. Before you strike, raise your right knee and plant your right foot firmly onto the floor. With your right foot planted into the floor, just go through the motions of the strike. You strike with the *little finger* side of your forearms.

Look at Figure 108. This shows the correct position of your forearms when you strike. As soon as you have made contact with his elbows, push hard into them as though you are trying to push them into each other, and keep pushing. All you have to do now is roll. Push your right foot hard into the floor and roll your body in an anti-clockwise direction. *Don't* release his arms when you are rolling; keep pushing them into each other. The outcome will be that the attacker will be forced head first onto the floor. Be very careful when you practise this escape method. You will have to release your partner's

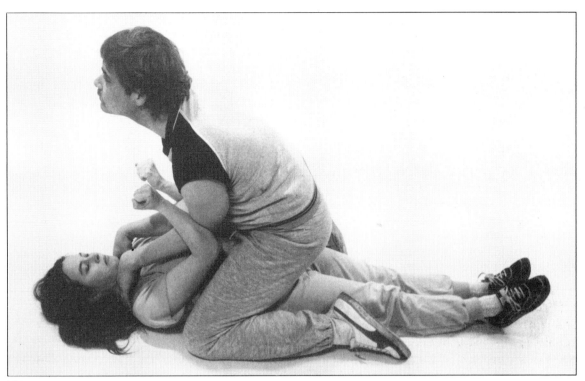

108

109

arms to save injury. If you *don't* want to release your partner's arms, then make sure that he/she has plenty of thick cushions to land on. It is much better to practise this escape method without releasing your partner because, if you get used to releasing the attacker before he hits the floor, then, in a real attack, you would release the attacker automatically and, although he would still have damaged elbows, you would not have the advantage of him being stunned. So make sure that you have plenty of cushions for your partner to land on, safely.

An important point to remember when using the rolling escape technique is always to roll away from the raised knee. If you want to roll to the left, you raise the right knee and *vice versa.*

SUMMARY

N.B. This summary assumes that you are going to roll your body anti-clockwise.

1. Raise your right knee and place your right foot firmly into the floor.

2. Strike both of your attacker's elbows at the same time with your forearms.

3. After striking your attacker's elbows with your forearms, keep pushing into his elbows as if to make your forearms meet.

4. Two movements: still pushing into your attacker's elbows with your forearms push down hard onto your right foot; roll your body anti-clockwise.

5. *Run.*

Floor (Arms Pinned) Escape No. 1

Look at Figure 110. This is one of the most frightening ways an attacker can pin you to the floor. The attacker has pinned his victim to the floor and has also locked her arms into the sides of her body. It seems almost impossible for the victim to be able to escape. Her arms are trapped and the attacker is trying to strangle her. Irrespective of how hopeless it looks, the victim can still escape.

Look at Figure 110 again. The victim has raised both of her knees and planted both of her feet firmly onto the floor.

Now look at Figure 111. The victim has raised her hips and the attacker is beginning to roll over the top of her head.

Look at Figure 112. The attacker has been forced completely over the top of the victim's head and has been thrown, head first onto the floor. As soon as the victim has thrown the attacker over the top of her head, she would naturally get away as fast as possible.

HOW TO PRACTISE

Get your partner to straddle you, as shown in Figure 110. Make certain that your arms are trapped into your sides, just as shown. Your partner should apply a stranglehold with both hands. Once the hold is applied, you can begin the escape.

The first thing to do is raise both of your knees and plant both of your feet firmly onto the floor. Figure 110 shows the correct position.

Now look at Figure 111. Thrust your hips upwards as the victim is doing. Make sure that your hands are placed in the same position as shown: on the attacker's bottom. As you thrust your hips upwards, use your hands and arms to help to throw the attacker over your head. Your hips, hands and arms all move at the same time.

Look at Figure 112. The attacker has been thrown completely over the head of the victim. When you are practising, make sure that your partner has plenty of pillows to land on. It may sound very easy, and indeed it is. The secret lies in the attacker's body weight distribution. If you look at Figure 110 again, you can see

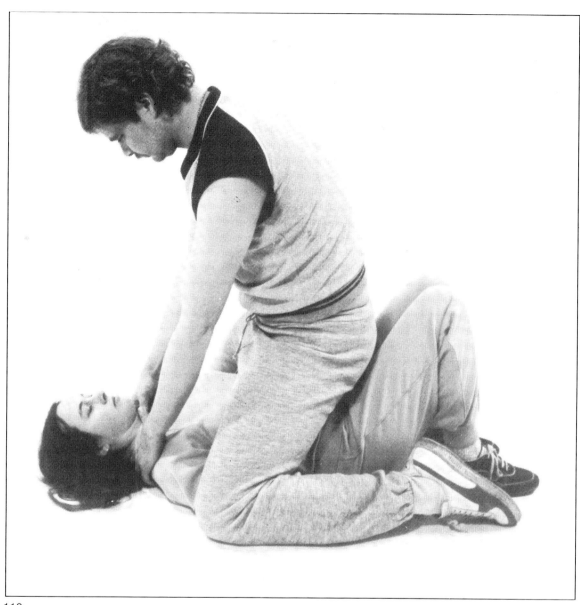

110

that the attacker is leaning down onto the victim's throat. All of his upper body weight is pushing downwards into the victim's throat rather than onto her hips, where he is sitting. By pushing your hips upwards, you are re-directing his weight over your head. If he doesn't release his grip on your throat, he'll be forced, head first, into the floor. The normal body reaction of the attacker to this escape method is to protect himself as he is thrown over, thus releasing his stranglehold.

One point to bear in mind about this escape method is that the attacker will probably not be stunned. He may well be shocked, but he is still capable of inflicting injury. So, as soon as you have thrown him over your head, get up and *run*.

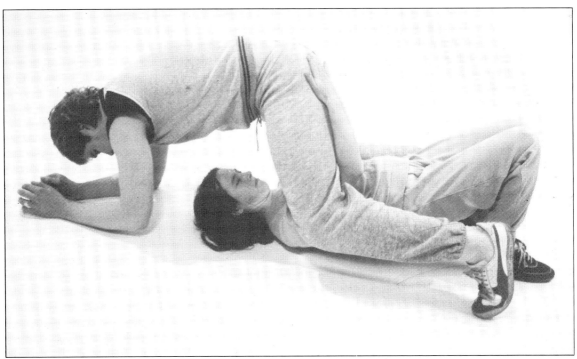

111

112

SUMMARY
1. Raise both of your knees and plant both feet firmly onto the floor.
2. Two movements: thrust upwards with your hips; push upwards on the attacker's bottom with both of your hands.
3. *Run.*

Floor (Arms Pinned) Escape No. 2

This next method employs the rolling method used earlier, but in a rather special way.

The attacker straddles his victim as shown in Figure 110. The victim's arms are trapped into her sides once again.

Now look at Figure 113. The victim has gripped the attacker's heel and has raised her bottom.

Now look at Figure 114. The attacker is being rolled off the victim's body and he is in extreme pain. He has released the stranglehold and is on his way to the floor.

HOW TO PRACTISE

This escape method can cause serious injury, so extreme caution should be taken when you practise. Don't try to rush through it; take your time and do it gently.

Get your partner to straddle you as shown in Figure 110. Your arms are trapped into your sides.

Now look at Figure 113. Raise your left hip and, at the same time, grip your attacker's right ankle/heel with your left hand. Now, pull your attacker's ankle/heel in towards your body so that the inside of his ankle is forced to the floor. As you are pulling the ankle/heel inwards, sit on it. That is why you raised your left hip. When practising with a partner, sit very carefully onto his heel. If you move too quickly, you may injure him. Once you sit onto the attacker's heel and the inside of his ankle is forced to the floor, raise your right knee and plant your right foot firmly onto the floor. Once you are in this position, the attacker may, or may not, be experiencing severe pain in either his ankle or knee. It depends on the fluidity of his ankles. Practise that part of the escape first. Be very careful, especially if your partner

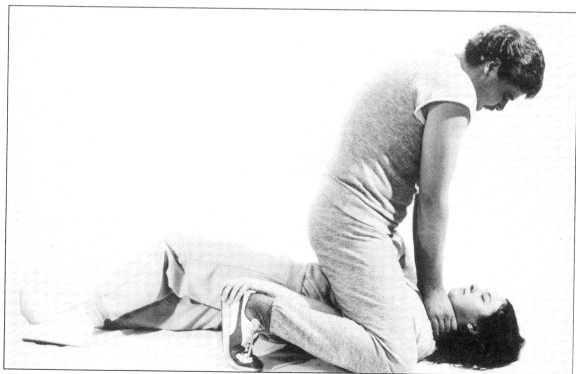

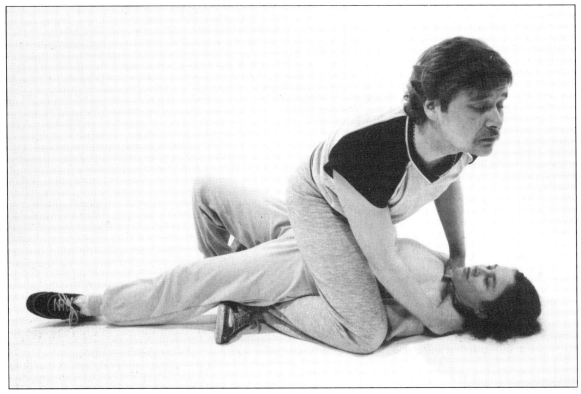

114

doesn't have much fluidity in his ankles. When you can move into this position fairly easily, you can go on to the final part of the escape.

The final part of this escape method is the roll. You should have the attacker's ankle trapped beneath your bottom and your right knee should be raised with your right foot planted firmly onto the floor. To roll to maximum efficiency, push your right foot hard into the floor and, keeping your left hip on top of the attacker's right ankle, roll in an anti-clockwise direction. If you are practising with a partner, roll *very slowly* and *stop* as soon as your partner tells you. If you don't stop, you *will* cause your partner severe injury. Obviously, in a real attack, it would be up to you. You could stop as soon as you hear the attacker's screams or, you could ignore the screams and injure him, maybe permanently. This escape method is so painful for the attacker because you are using his own weight to inflict his injury. It is something like an arm lock really. You are forcing his joints to work against themselves. Check it out for

yourself. Look at your own legs. Your knees are designed to bend, not to twist or rotate. Your ankles are designed to bend and, to some extent, twist. Now, by sitting on the attacker's ankle, you are twisting and bending it. When you roll, you are forcing his knee to twist/rotate. That is what causes the extreme pain. Should the attacker try to stand while you were sitting on his ankle, the pain in his knee would worsen because he would be twisting/rotating his knee. In like manner, should he try to roll away from you, the outcome would be the same; he would twist/rotate his knee.

In a real attack, the faster you roll, the better, but it is no use rolling if you haven't trapped his ankle first.

Don't forget the rule for the rolling escape method. Roll *away* from the raised knee.

Once you have practised the escape as I've described, try it from the other side of your body. Grip his ankle with your right hand and raise your left knee, etc.

A final word of advice concerning this escape method. As soon as the attacker has been rolled off your body, don't wait to see how much damage you've done. Get away and get help. You may not be injured, but the attacker probably is.

SUMMARY

N.B. This summary assumes you are going to roll your body anti-clockwise.

1. Two movements: raise you left hip; grip the attacker's right ankle/heel with your left hand.

2. Two movements: pull the attacker's ankle/heel towards your body; lower your raised left hip onto your attacker's ankle/heel so that the inside of his ankle is being forced to the floor.

3. Two movements: push down hard into the floor with your right foot; roll your body anti-clockwise forcing the attacker to the floor.

4. *Run.*

CONCLUSION

If you find that you *are* pinned to the floor during an attack. Then one thing is for sure, everything you've tried so far has failed. No matter what the reason, you are on the floor with the attacker on top. But you still have a chance to escape if you have read and practised carefully all I have tried to teach you in this chapter. Some of the escape methods described may seem a little harsh but your attacker is also being harsh and the chances are that he is much bigger and stronger than you. If you find yourself in this situation, then it is probably going to be the last chance you will get to escape. If you really want to escape, then you must be harsh. You are going to be raped, if you don't escape *now!* As always, only *you* can decide. You are the one that is being attacked. Of course, if you feel that you can escape without being harsh, then that's fine. I hope you succeed, but somehow I doubt it. You see, the women I have spoken to who have been raped, didn't have the advantage of knowing any self defence techniques. Once they were pinned to the floor, they believed that there was nothing else they could do. They nearly always struggled and fought back but, once on the floor, they gave in. They all said the same thing. If only they had known how to stun their attacker, just for a few seconds they could have escaped. It is their testimonies that made me decide which methods to include in this chapter.

It takes a long time to recover from a *failed* rape attack. A successful one is a life sentence.

13 Personal Security and Travel

A woman who travels alone late at night obviously hasn't read the advice given in Chapter 1. Nor has the woman who accepts a lift from a stranger or a man she knows only slightly. If women were generally just a little more security-minded, it would prevent so many attacks. Obviously there are times when you have no alternative. You either accept a lift or you travel alone. This being the case, it makes sense to know how you can lessen the odds against attack.

In the modern world, we have come to expect a little comfort when we travel. That comfort usually comes in the shape of a seat or chair. Road, rail, air or boat, we expect to have a seat. Being seated doesn't mean that you are safe from attack. On the contrary, being seated puts you in a far more vulnerable position. You are more vulnerable because you are more relaxed when you are sitting down. How many times have you seen someone asleep on a train or bus? Perhaps you have dozed off yourself when you have been coming home from work? If you have, then you will understand what I mean about being more vulnerable when you are seated.

Apart from hijacking and acts of war, attacks against women who travel by air are very rare. It really is true what the airlines tell us: 'It's the safest way to travel'. Unfortunately, the same cannot be said for women who travel by bus, tube/subway or train.

Travelling by Bus

If you are forced to travel alone at night, or any other time for that matter, there are certain things you *can* do, which, in the event of a personal attack, will make it easier to escape or avoid the attack. For instance, if it's late at night and you have to take the bus home, sit close to the driver where you can be seen. In doing this, a would-be attacker runs the risk of being seen by a witness. An attacker doesn't want to be seen for fear of being caught. Sitting close to the driver also has the added advantage of having help close to hand should you need it. As you board the bus, look for the passengers' bell/buzzer. If you know where it is situated, then once again you can attract attention to yourself if necessary. Make sure that you can see the doors clearly. If you can see the doors, then you can spot any undesirable characters as soon as they board. If you are not certain how much the fare is to your destination, keep your voice down and ask very quietly how much it is. If an attacker knows where you are alighting he could very easily stand up to get off before you do. You wouldn't feel threatened by this. Seeing another passenger stand up to alight before you would appear normal. If he doesn't know where you are going he can't fool you!

If your intuition tells you that another passenger is a threat, then try to discover if you are right. Stand up to alight three or four stops before your destination. If your intuition is correct, the potential attacker should get up to follow you. All you have to do then is say you're sorry it's the wrong stop and sit down again. If the potential attacker sits down making the same excuses it could be a coincidence. So do it again. If he follows you again then the chances are that your intuition is correct. Your next course of action should be to tell the driver that you are frightened and why.

One of the women from my classes did exactly as I have just described. The driver, being a married man, understood the woman's fear. He stopped the bus and approached the other passenger. The driver asked him where he was getting off. The passenger said he was getting off at the next stop, which he did. The woman was delighted. Naturally she was pretty shaken up to think that she could have been attacked. But she wasn't.

Whether the man on the bus would have attacked the woman or not is anyone's guess. One thing is certain. If the man *was* an attacker then he didn't attack *this* woman. She kept her wits about her and used good old-fashioned commonsense to avoid what might have been a very dangerous situation.

SUMMARY

1. If you don't know how much the fare is to your destination, ask very quietly.
2. Look for the passenger's buzzer/bell and make a mental note where it is situated.
3. Sit close to the driver.
4. Make sure you can see the doors clearly.
5. If you feel threatened by another passenger, get up to alight three or four stops *before* your destination.
6. If the person that worries you mirrors your actions more than once, tell the driver.
7. If it's late at night and there is nobody to meet you at your destination, walk quickly and confidently in the centre of the pavement/sidewalk. Try and stay where it is well lit. Avoid dimly-lit short cuts and try to stay in the crowd.

Travelling by Tube or Subway

Women who travel alone late at night on the tube/subway or on trains are not being very sensible. It is much safer to use a taxi cab. The precautions you can take are much fewer than for a bus. But, for the foolhardy, these few things might help.

When you are in a situation in which you fear you may be followed (e.g. leaving a train or platform where a man has been watching you), wait until he has gone or boarded a train rather than rushing to be first.

Try not to sit in an empty carriage. It is much safer to stay in a crowd. When you are in the carriage, sit close to the emergency stop lever/chain, or close to the guard's van. Try to sit where you can see the rest of the compartment.

SUMMARY

1. Try to take a taxi cab rather than use the tube/subway.
2. Do not rush to be first.
3. Stay in the crowd.
4. Sit close to the emergency stop lever/chain, or guard's van.
5. Sit where you can see the rest of the compartment.

Travelling by Car: Driving

If you drive your own car you should ensure that door locks and windows are in good working order. When driving alone, lock your doors and windows. Don't give lifts to anyone you don't know very well. Under no circumstances give lifts to strangers or men you know only slightly. It's better to be safe than sorry.

If you ever feel that you are being followed by another car, try to stay in an area you know very well. Drive in a circle so that you arrive back where you started. In doing this, you will know if you really are being followed. If you are, then drive to the nearest Police station. If there isn't a Police station or precinct near, then attract attention to yourself. Sound the horn, flash the lights and, if your car is fitted with hazard warning or pass lights, switch them on. All of these things will attract attention. If the trailing car *is* being driven by a potential attacker, then chances are he doesn't want to be seen or get noticed. He'll want to get away from you just as much as you want him to go away. Don't forget to take his registration number. The car owner can be easily traced once the police have the number.

SUMMARY

1. Make sure that door locks and windows are in good working order.
2. Always lock the doors and windows when you drive alone.
3. Never give lifts to strangers or people you don't know very well.
4. If you are being followed, drive in a circle and then to the nearest Police station.
5. If no Police station is near by, then attract attention to yourself. Sound the horn etc.

6. Take the registration number of the offending car and report it to the Police.

Travelling By Car: As a Passenger

You should never accept lifts from strangers or men you know only slightly but, if you are going to be a passenger in a car, there are certain things that you should find out as soon as you get in.

The first thing is how to open the door. Ask where the door catch is and ask how to operate it. (You could make the excuse that you have caught your coat or dropped some money.) You should also find out how to unfasten the seat belts and how to open and close the windows. If you know these few things then, should you be attacked, you will know how to release the seat belt quickly and how to get out in a hurry.

If an attacker were to have 'roaming hands' while the car is moving, then knowing how to open the windows could help to stop him. All you need do is open the window and shout for help. Your shouting would attract attention to the car. Tell him that, if he doesn't stop, you'll carry on shouting.

One woman told me of an attack similar to the one I have just described. She acted just as I have suggested, but the driver continued to molest her. Not to be beaten, she unfastened her seat belt, raised her knee, then kicked at the windscreen. The attacker removed his hands immediately. He stopped the car and climbed out to inspect the damage. The woman was in no real danger. She didn't try to run. You see, the attacker was her husband! Her actions almost caused a divorce, but she believes that this kind of retaliation would stop any man from continuing with this type of attack. She bases her theory on the fact that most of the men she knows care more for their cars than anything else in the world. The windscreen didn't shatter, but she tells me that it does leak every time it rains.

I've told you about this case because it is a very good example of thinking for yourself. In a genuine attack situation, the chances are that you will be alone with the attacker. Then you must think for yourself. As always, you'll be on your own!

SUMMARY
1. Ask where the door catch is and find out how it works.
2. Find out how to unfasten the seat belts.
3. Ask how to open and close the windows.

Walking

Just about everybody in the Western world has, at some time, had to walk home late at night. For whatever reason, we have all had to do it. If we care to ask ourselves *why* we walked home, we would soon discover that it was not necessary. It could have been avoided in most circumstances. With just a little forethought that 'late night walk' could be avoided.

If you know that you are likely to be late, get somebody to meet you or call a cab. Even if you have no money with you, the fare can always be paid at your destination. Of course, the easiest way to avoid the 'late night walk' is to make sure you leave in plenty of time to catch the next to last bus. (Should you miss this one, you can still catch the last one). So, assuming that you have caught the next to last bus, you are still going to have to walk home from the bus stop.

Walking home from a bus stop has caused many hearts to miss a beat. However, there are certain precautions you can take to lessen the odds against attack. To begin with, as soon as you step off the bus, it is a good idea to look up and down the street to see who, if anyone, is around. In doing this, you can avoid a confrontation with anyone you don't like the look of. Walk in the centre of the pavement. If there should be an attacker lurking in a shop doorway then at least you will have a couple of paces to start your running escape. You should walk briskly and confidently. If you look confident this can sometimes be enough to keep a would-be attacker at bay.

If you see somebody hanging around a street corner and you feel uncertain about him, cross over the road. If the person you are unsure of also crosses over then you will have time to take evasive action.

If you think you are being followed, don't be afraid to have a look. You can very easily look behind you without the follower knowing. Use your peripheral vision. All you have to do is pretend to cough. As you raise your hand to cover your mouth, turn your head sideways and have a look. We very often think we are being followed at night when in fact we are not. Sound travels much further at night and it could be that you are hearing footsteps in the next street. It could even be your imagination playing tricks on you because you feel a bit edgy. So have a look!

If you are being followed by someone you don't recognise then you have several alternatives. You could try to find out their intentions by crossing the road. If the follower also crosses the road, then cross back to the other side. By doing this you will eliminate coincidence. If the follower also crosses back to the other side of the road, the chances are that he *is* following you. You can also be pretty sure that he knows you have spotted him. This being the case then he'll probably do one of two things: go for you or make a quick exit. You'll know if he is going to attack you by the sound of his feet. His pace will quicken. If this is the case, then run to the nearest front door and bang on it as hard as you can. Don't forget to shout *fire* as you bang on the door. When an attacker sees lights going on and people taking an interest in what is going on he will normally run off to avoid capture.

An alternative, which you can use when you believe you are being followed, is to increase the distance between you and the follower. You can do this without the follower knowing. This is how it's done. Suppose you are walking briskly and confidently. You have looked behind to see who is following you and you can hear the sound of your own footsteps as well as those of the follower. Now, time your own footsteps. Let us assume that you are walking at about five paces every 4 seconds. If the distance covered with each step is, say, 3 feet, then you are covering 15 feet for every five paces you take. Now, if you increase your stride to say 3 feet and 6 inches, you will cover 17 feet and 6 inches for every five paces. So for ten paces, you have added a further 5 feet between you and the follower. The secret is to do it without him knowing. That is why you timed your paces. You don't have to use a watch to time your paces. Just make a mental note of the time: one-two-three-four, one-two-three-four, etc. Once you have the timing in your head, you can increase the length of your stride. When you increase the length of your stride you must maintain the same rhythm (one-two-three-four, etc). You have to listen for the sound of the follower's footsteps so that you can judge for yourself whether or not he is following you. If he is following you, then you will hear the pace of his strides increase when he realises you are making ground. He'll have no idea how you made ground, so if he wants to attack you he will have to catch you up. If you have walked forty paces before he realises that you are much further away, then he has a lot of catching up to do. (e.g. forty increased strides equals another 20 feet between you and the follower). You will have the extra distance, and time, to take evasive action.

Many women who are forced to walk home late at night (barmaids, croupiers, cinema usherettes, etc.) have asked me whether I believe it a good idea to carry some type of weapon. My answer is always the same. 'If you carry a weapon you may find yourself in trouble with the Police. If you carry a weapon, then sooner or later you will be tempted to use it'. It's not much of an answer, but it is the only one I can give without getting into trouble with the Police myself! I never recommend the carriage of known weapons, guns, knives etc. If you don't know how to use them you might end up getting shot or stabbed yourself.

Because of this dilemma with weapons, I feel that I must tell you about an everyday item which can be very effective in shocking an attacker during the hours of darkness – a box of matches! If you hold the box in one hand and three or four matches in the other then, should you be attacked, it is not too difficult to strike and throw the ignited matches into the face of the attacker. If you have ever dropped a lighted match in your lap you will understand how much panic it creates. So what do you think three or four matches thrown into an attacker's face would do to him? He will be shocked and temporarily blinded, giving you the extra seconds you need to get away.

It's very important that you throw the matches as soon as you strike them. Strike, then throw them as they flare. If you strike and wait, they will probably go out before you throw them and extinguished matches are not much use. Hold the matches so that the heads are all together, otherwise only one or two will flare when you strike them. Hold the heads together and they will all burst into flame at the same time, giving you valuable time in which to make your escape.

SUMMARY

1. Look up and down the street to see who is around.

2. Walk quickly and confidently in the centre of the pavement.

3. If you are uncertain of somebody who is ahead of you, cross the road.

4. If you think you are being followed, have a look.

5. If you think somebody behind you is following you, cross the road to see if you are followed. Then cross back again to double check.

5a. (Alternative) Increase the distance between you and the follower. Time your paces. Increase the length of your stride.

6. If the follower goes for you, bang on the nearest door shouting *fire!*

7. Matches. Hold three or four matches so that their heads are together. Hold the matches in one hand, the box in the other. If attacked, strike the matches and throw them into the face of the attacker. Throw the matches as soon as they flare.

Conclusion

Normally, at the end of each course, the women who attend want to know how effective their newfound skills really are. So I bring in the male beginners from my martial arts school. These young men have not been taught the methods I teach on the courses, so the women have surprise on their side. I get the beginners to attack the women in various ways and tell the women to escape, using the methods they have been taught on the course.

The men who come along to attack the women are all volunteers, but they seldom volunteer twice! To date, the Ladies' Self Defence Association has an impeccable safety record – none of the women attending our courses have ever been injured. Fortunately, the same cannot be said for the men who 'attack' them. The women always manage to escape and get away.

My volunteers are usually in their late teens or early twenties and have been practising martial arts for about 2 to 3 months. So they are young and strong, fit and healthy, and very confident. They come along thinking it's just going to be a bit of fun. I almost always feel very guilty. I know what the women are going to do to them. I know that these fit and strong young men are about to have their confidence shattered. I know, that these women *are* going to escape and get away from their attackers and that, afterwards I shall have to rebuild the shattered egos and replace the lost confidence of the men.

It is not a job I enjoy, but it does help these young men to understand what a rape attack means to a woman. Many of the young men, while they nurse their shattered egos send their wives, girlfriends and mothers to the next available course. They do this because they have firsthand knowledge that a woman *can* escape from a rapist.

The credit for the women escaping from their would-be attackers is not mine for creating the course. The credit belongs to the women themselves, because they did something positive. They all recognised the necessity to learn: 'If you decide to fight make it count'. All of the women who attend the course have been taught the same escape methods covered in this book. If they can escape from an attacker after completing the course, then you should be able to also. The women who attend the course have done exactly what you have done but they didn't have the benefit of this book to refer to. Now that you have read the book and done something positive about the major social problem we call 'The Rape Problem' it would be sensible to start practising, wouldn't it? Even if you only practise once or twice a week, then that is far more than other people are doing. If you forget one or two things while you are practising, then you will have the book at hand to remind you. That is something which the women who attended our early courses didn't have. *You* don't have to forget. You have the book to remind you. If you keep on practising, everything you have learned will be kept in your mind, clean as a new pin. It will be there ready to get you out of trouble whenever the need arises.

You may be wondering if there is anything more that you can do to prevent the possibility of a rape attack. Well, in short, there is no simple answer. But there are some things, which may *eventually* reduce this inhumane crime. I suppose the first thing to do is to find a cure for that modern disease, *apathy*. As long as people cease to care, women will continue to be raped. On every day, of every week, of every year, women get raped. Women everywhere must understand that it is foolhardy to believe it couldn't happen to them. It can, and does, happen. People must learn to stop thinking that it always happens to somebody else. There are thousands of 'somebody elses' every year.

So, what can you do to help? Well, by talking to your friends for a start. Perhaps writing to people in authority will help – your MP, perhaps your local Police station, doctors or social workers – in fact anyone in authority will do. If enough women show their outrage, then *eventually* something *must* surely be done. Perhaps you could organise a pressure group or a petition. In Great Britain, there are two women's groups in particular which are trying to do something positive: one is 'Rape Crisis', and the other is 'Women against Rape'. Both groups are voluntary. If you live in Great Britain perhaps you could offer your services to one of these groups. If you live outside Great Britain, why not form your own group. Even talking to the men you know can help. Enough women telling the macho male that his attitude is dangerous *can* help to change that attitude. That there seems to be two standards of morality is unjust; we all know it. So if you press hard enough you could change these dangerous attitudes.

The problems can *eventually* be reduced, but it's going to take time and effort. *Eventually* seems to be a key word that comes up far too often. It seems that, until these *eventualities* come into being, the only positive thing to do is *defend* yourself. Until the Police and our Governments can find some concrete solutions, we are going to continue to suffer from the crimes of the rapists. We shall have to continue telling our children not to talk to strange men and I, with the help of my colleagues, will continue to teach how 'if you decide to fight, to make it count'.

Many years ago, as a very young martial arts student, I was given a simple philosophy to study. The beauty within it is beyond question. I have, since devoting my time to researching the rape epidemic, found it increasingly difficult to accept its message. But I shall not allow my rage to come to the fore. Instead, I shall continue to learn from this, the greatest lesson I have ever been taught!

Avoid rather than check,
Check rather than hurt,
Hurt rather than maim,
Maim rather than kill,
For all life is sacred,
And once taken, cannot be replaced.

GOOD LUCK

Index

Figures in *italics* refer to pages
bearing line illustrations. Figures in
bold refer to black and white plate
numbers.

Arm holds   90–102, **58–60**
Arm holds (arms down)
   escapes   90–95, **58**
      step and elbow strike   93–95
      95, **62–63**
      twisting out   91–93, *93*, **61**
Arm holds (arms up) escapes,
   throwing   90, 96–98, **59,**
   64–66
Arm holds (two arms against one)
   escapes   90, 98–102
      finger or thumb bending
      100–102, *60*, **69–70**
      pulling out   98–100, **67–68**
Arm lock application   56–58,
   106–108, **74–75**
Attack, lessening the chances of
   12
Awareness   11–14

Bear hugs   76–89, **46, 50**
Bear hugs (front) escapes   76–80
   knee and stamp   78
   pinching   78
   throwing   79–80, **47–49**
   tickling   76

Bear hugs (rear) escapes   80–89
   finger or thumb bending
      82–84, **51**
   pinch, hammerfist, or
      chop/knifehand   80–82
   see-saw   86–89, **55–57**
   shock/stun
      (groin/feet)   84–85
   throwing 85–86, **52–54**

Conclusions   155–156
   arm holds   102
   arm locks   108
   hugs   89
   floor holds   149
   kicks   50
   pulling attacks   132
   running escapes   55
   strangles   75
   walking escapes   64
   wall holds   118
   wrist locks   108

Flashers   12
Floor holds   133–149, **99**
Floor holds escapes
   leg scissors   137–139,
      103–104
   wrist lock   133–136, **100–102**
Floor strangles (arms free)
   escapes   139–144, **105**
      simultaneous striking
         143–144, **108–109**
      wrist and arm lock   139–142,
         106–107

Floor strangles (arms pinned)
   escapes   144–149, **110**
      rolling out   147–149,
         113–114
      throwing   144–147, **111–112**
Free-standing holds *see* Arm
   holds; Arm locks; Bear hugs;
   Strangles; Wrist locks

Handbag snatchers   12

Kicks   38–50
   back   46–50, **12–16**
   front   38–41, **1–3**
   roundhouse   41–43, **4–7**
   step through side   43–46,
      8–11

Ladies Self Defence
   Association   7–9

Personal security   150–156
Practice
   arm holds (arms down)
      escapes   91, 93, 95
   arm holds (arms up)
      escapes   96–97
   arm holds (two against one)
      escape   98, 101
   arm lock application   106,
      108

bear hugs (front) escapes
76, 78, 80
bear hugs (rear) escapes
82, 84, 85, 86, 87–88
floor hold escapes
136, 137–139
floor strangles (arms free)
escapes 139, 142, 144
floor strangles (arms pinned)
escapes 144–145, 147–149
kick, back 46–49
kick, front 40
kick, roundhouse 42–43
kick, step through side
45–46
pulling attack (by feet)
escape 126, 127, 128
pulling attack (by wrists)
escape 131
pulling attack (single arm)
escape 124–126
pulling attack (two arm)
escapes 120–121, 121–122
running escape 52–55
strangles (bent arm)
escapes 72, 73, 74
strangles (straight arm)
escapes 68, 70, 71–72
walking escapes 58, 61, 63
wall hold (body) escape 111
wall hold (facing the wall)
escapes 116, 117, 118
wall hold (single arm)
escape 114
wall hold (strangle) 113–114
wrist lock application
103, 105
Pulling attacks 119–132
Pulling attack (by the feet)
escape 126–129, **93–95**
Pulling attack (by the wrists)
escape 129–132, **96–98**
Pulling attack (single arm) escape,
side kick 122–126, **90–92**

Pulling attack (two arm) escapes
119–122, **87**
knee strike 119–121, **88**
pushing 121–122, **89**

Rape attackers 12
Rape incidence in
UK 11
USA 11
Rape, convictions for 13
Reactions to attack 51
Running escapes 51–55, **17–22**

Strangles 65–75 *see below and also*
Floor strangles; Wallhold
(strangle)
Strangles (bent arm) escapes 65,
72–74, **33**
double pull 73–74, **44, 45**
heels of hands to ears 73
knee strike to groin 72–73
Strangles (straight arm) escapes
65–66, **32**
arms trapping 68–70, **38–40**
finger bending 66–68, **34–37**
'S' 70—72, **41–43**
Summaries
arm holds 93, 95, 97–98,
100, 102
arm locks 108
bear hugs 76, 77, 78, 80, 82,
84, 85, 86, 89
floor holds 136, 139, 142,
144, 147, 149
kicks 41, 43, 46, 49–50
pulling attacks 121, 122,
126, 128, 132
running escape 55
strangles 68, 70, 72, 73, 74,
142, 144, 147, 149
walking escapes 58, 61, 63
wall holds 111, 114,
116, 118
wrist locks 105

Travelling precautions
bus 150–151
car 151–152
tube (subway) 151
walking 152–154

Use of this book 10

Walking, precautions 152–154
Walking escapes 56–64
arm lock 56–58, **23–26**
elbow strike 58–61, **27–28**
side kick 61–63, **29–31**
Wall holds 109–118, **76**
Wall hold (body) escape,
throwing 109–111, **76–78**
Wall hold (facing the wall)
escapes 115–118
tummy gap 116–118, **83, 86**
twist and elbow strike
115–116, **83–85**
Wall hold (single arm)
escape 114, **82**
Wall hold (strangle) escape, arms
folding 111–114, **79–81**

Warming up exercises 15–37
arms and shoulders 22, *22*
back stretching 32, *32*
backward leg stretching
36, *36*
balance 28, *28*, 29, *29*
cardiovascular 23, *23*
complementary stretching
37, *37*
co-ordination 24, *24*
cross bends 25, *25*
doggy sit ups 31, *31*
forward leg stretching
34, *34*
hips loosening 37, *37*

jumping on the spot   16, *16*
knees   26, *26,* 27, *27*
neck   21, *21*
push ups   29, *29*
sideways stretching   32, *32*
sit ups   30, *30*

spinal stretching   32, *32*
squats   18, *18*
squat stretches   27, *27*
stand ups   33, *33*
star jumps   17, *17*
toe touching   24, *24*

torso rounds   26, *26*
waist and back   20, *20*
waist stretching   19, *19*
Weapons   153
Wrist lock application   103–105,
   72–73